ADD/ONS

ADD/ONS

IMAGINATIVE AND RESOURCEFUL DESIGNS FOR EXPANDING KITCHENS, BEDROOMS, BATHROOMS, AND LIVING SPACE

by Kenneth Lelen

G. P. PUTNAM'S SONS / NEW YORK

For my son, Ian

Frontispiece: Family room addition to a suburban tract house.
Designed by Stan Better.

Library of Congress Cataloging in Publication Data

Lelen, Kenneth.
  Add-ons.

  1. Dwellings—Remodeling—Designs and plans.   I. Title.
NA7125.L43   1984   728.3'7'0286   84-3424
ISBN 0-399-12917-0

Printed in Singapore

CONTENTS

Introduction 7

SUN SPACES AND GREENHOUSES

1. **Curved Sun Room Brightens Adobe Home** 11
2. **Oriel Brings Light and View to Victorian Dining Room** 15
3. **Farmhouse Renovation Adds Studio and Greenhouse** 18
4. **Seaside Space for Home Hobbyists** 23
5. **Guest House Matches Adobe-Style Home** 28
6. **A New Angle on Suburban Living** 32
7. **Greenhouse Brightens City House Interiors** 37
8. **A Sunny Addition for Family Entertaining** 40

KITCHENS AND DINING AREAS

9. **Oak-trimmed Addition Replaces Austere Kitchen** 44
10. **Facilities Expanded for Efficient Entertaining** 48
11. **Kitchen Expansion Updates Town House** 51
12. **''Bump Out'' Forms Cook's New Space** 54
13. **Making Room for More Than One Cook** 57
14. **Gazebo Inspires New Breakfast Room** 61

MAJOR ADDITIONS—BEDROOMS, LIVING ROOMS, AND FAMILY ROOMS

15. **Relocated Entry Invites New Look at Old House** 65
16. **Summer Bungalow Raised to New Heights** 69
17. **Weekend House Mirrors River Views** 72
18. **This Old Building Serves Many New Functions** 77
19. **Cottage Addition Makes Room for Summer Guests** 82
20. **Renovation and Addition Form One New Structure** 87
21. **Dolphin Marks Entry to New Guest Suite** 90
22. **Cherished Home for a New Generation** 94
23. **Existing Plan Reworked for More Usable Space** 99
24. **Renovation Demonstrates Energy-Saving Methods** 103

EXTERIOR AND SPECIAL PURPOSE ADD-ONS

25. **A Pig with a Purple Eye Patch** 108
26. **Whimsical ''Foliage'' Enhances Entryway** 112
27. **Boathouse Expands Lakeside Pleasures** 115
28. **Instant Landscaping Makes Lasting Impression** 118
29. **Hexagonal Design Satisfies Revised Expectations** 122
30. **Music Inspires Dramatic Pavillion** 126

Project Specifications 131
Add-On Source Directory 145
Acknowledgments and Photo Credits 159

INTRODUCTION

There was a time not so long ago when you just moved on to a different house when a major change in life style occurred. Another child in the family? The answer, pocket book allowing, was probably to find a larger home. And when growing children required rooms of their own, the solution was often to seek a new home rather than to enlarge the old. Even after children had gone out on their own and the special interests of the parents assumed more importance, a home designed originally for family living was frequently left behind for an easier-to-care-for model. Finding a new home has never been an easy task, but when interest rates on mortgages were low and the housing stock plentiful, trading up in real estate was a national pastime. Today, remodeling a home to meet new needs makes more economic sense than starting all over at a higher cost. A creatively designed addition, known in the building trade as an add-on, can measurably enlarge not only your sense of space but also the equity earned in home ownership.

But if you're looking for an easy way to add space to your home, forget it. Adding on can be a long and difficult process that takes more time and money than most people expect. That's the bad news.

The good news is that hiring an experienced architect can save you time, money, and headaches. In this book you will see how thirty residential additions were developed with the assistance of professional designers. The book offers inventive design ideas and practical working methods that other home owners have used to gain space, comfort, and utility.

Why work with an architect on an add-on project? Because you will want someone to pay strict attention to your individual needs and desires, budget, life style, routine, imagination, physical requirements, and a host of personal wishes that are important to you.

How do you find the right architect? One of the best ways to locate an architect for an add-on project is to ask other home owners who have recently remodeled their houses. Local chapters of the American Institute of Architects (AIA), kitchen dealers who work with certified kitchen designers (CKDs), local preservation groups, and many state historic preservation offices can also refer you to (but not recommend) reputable architects.

Look for someone who has had experience with residential addition projects. These professionals know what floor-plan quirks are easily solved, which materials will stand up to daily use or the scouring abuse of the weather, how you can accomplish your objectives in stages you can afford, how to create a dramatic effect in a room, how to expand a space without moving walls, and how to manage the subcontractors on the job site.

Compile a list of candidates and call or write each one. Be prepared to outline briefly the type and size of your project. At this stage it's too early to ask for sketches, cost estimates, or fee schedules. Instead, you should request references from the architects' previous clients. Call these people and ask them about their experience in working with the architects. Go see their completed add-ons if you can. A former client's comments will be as important as the architect's credentials and job experience.

You should meet with all the architects on your list. Some people prefer to meet at the house, while others set up a more formal introduction at the firm's office. In either case, you will want to hear polished presentations that describe their services, experience, and fees. At the same time, the architect will want to learn about you and your project. Allow enough time at these meetings so that you feel confident about each architect's methods, background, and expertise. If you are uncertain of your goals, say so. It's unlikely that you'll have all your ideas developed. That's the architect's job.

Add-on projects are usually twice as expensive as you think they might be, and take longer than owners expect, so you should never hesitate to ask architects to explain their design fees and services. You should also let the architect know your potential budget for the construction portion of your addition. Often it is possible to tailor the scope of the project to suit your budget.

No two architectural firms are alike; each one will offer you different suggestions. Use the interview to form an opinion about each firm and what it can do for you. Let the other firms know of your decision, and begin negotiations with the architect you select.

Architects charge for their services in several ways. A *lump sum* plan is often used on short-term jobs such as old-house inspection, energy audits, or when an architect agrees to provide only design drawings. A *cost plus* plan is frequently used by consultants and engineers to cover hourly or daily personnel expenses. Most architects use a *percentage of construction cost* plan for add-on projects. The fee usually varies between eight and fifteen percent of construction costs, but it can go as high as twenty percent. The billing procedure and a schedule of payments will be written up in a contract between you and the architect. Initially, five to ten percent of the total fee is paid as a retainer, with the remainder paid on a monthly basis or in percentages at established stages, with the balance due at the completion of the job.

An architect's services usually make up only a small part of your project's total cost. Many people have unrealistic ideas about the cost of an add-on and only learn about design fees and construction costs by talking to other home owners. Consequently, you should be clear and direct about the amount of money you plan to spend. If you can't arrive at a specific figure, it's a good idea to tell your architect that you might be willing to spend, say, $25,000 for your project, but not $35,000. This doesn't commit you to spending $25,000, yet it ensures that you won't spend more than that amount.

Who's in charge of the design of your residential add-on? The architect is responsible for the design and planning of the project, but you are ultimately responsible for everything that happens to the structure. Therefore, as owner, you have several obligations to the architect and the project.

For instance, you and your architect will work together to define and organize your requirements. The architect's job is to help you express your ideas and to develop a program that incorporates space requirements, critical needs, desirable goals, and personal objectives.

You may have to study your house in a new light, using unfamiliar language and strange new tools. Simply put, adding on to your house should be an educational project. This may be difficult, since most people don't have to think about renovation design problems on a daily basis. That's the architect's job.

You may even learn how to read sketches and drawings, land surveys, and other architectural documents. Be prepared to contribute your own time for research, discussions, and job-site decisions.

Generally speaking, your architect will be interested in your ideas but not in your solutions to design problems. Architects have the training, experience, and talent to solve challenging problems. You might have to step out of the way at times to let your architect do what is best for the structure. In short, flexibility (of your ego, too) is a key asset during the design phase.

During the rough stages of the design, you should let your imagination run free. It's *your* home. You should examine your own notions of what kind of addition you really want. What should it *feel* like to live there? Who is there with you in that space? What memories or pictures from the past does this imaginative space engender for you? To help you consider your thoughts and feelings about the addition you're planning, go to the library and check out a copy of *A Pattern Language* by Christopher Alexander, Sara Ishikawa, and Murray Silverstein (Oxford University Press, New York, 1977). It catalogues numerous building elements and describes how people react (through sight, touch, and perception) to their surroundings.

At some point your architect will make several rough sketches of the functions and building elements required for the project. These plans will be revised and refined until one or more satisfactory solutions are achieved. The architect will then present several design alternatives to you. Your responses are essential to the design process. You may see numerous versions of the project design as it develops. Don't be afraid or embarrassed to ask questions, criticize the plans, or demand to know the reasons for anything that you do not understand. You can request a preliminary estimate of construction costs at this stage, but don't expect any hard and fast figures.

Eventually, your architect will prepare detailed drawings that illustrate all aspects of the proposed addition. This is one of the toughest points in the design phase: you'll be asked to approve on paper what later will be built. Review these drawings carefully. They should thoroughly satisfy your original program and budget estimates. Ask hard questions and expect honest answers.

Once you've approved the drawings, your architect will prepare construction documents showing what the final structure will look like and what materials will be used. Contractors and craftsmen use copies of these working drawings and specifications to prepare their bids for construction labor and building materials. These documents are also presented to your town's building department for approval and permits.

10   The contractor and craftsmen you hire must build exactly what your architect has drawn on the construction documents. This may sound easy, but it's often the source of many job-site disagreements. Your architect may refer you to several contractors who can bid on the job. In many cases architects today run design-build firms. These companies not only provide the professional design services just described, but are also complete construction businesses in themselves. They can sometimes help you keep costs affordable and reduce job-site confusion since you're working with a familiar person who in turn is working for your interests.

In a competitive bidding situation, the lowest responsible bidder usually is selected. A negotiated contract, however, is sometimes preferable on special jobs. You and your architect should screen several contractors in advance and establish a list of acceptable bidders. Then you can either accept the lowest bidder or interview the contractors and select the one who best meets your requirements.

Your architect will function as your eyes and ears during the construction of your add-on, checking that work is proceeding on schedule and in accordance with the construction documents. But the architect does not actually supervise the construction work. That is the contractor's duty and responsibility. In practice, however, your architect should visit the job site often to observe the work, interpret the plans and specifications, and monitor the quality of the workmanship.

To prevent chaos and to preserve your sanity, all dealings between you and your contractor or craftsmen should be made through your architect. An architect can insist on corrections and changes in a more forceful manner than an owner, who doesn't always know what a "good" job or proper construction methods are.

As work progresses, your architect will document the completion of various construction phases and certify that payments should be made. Before the project is completed and the contractor leaves the job, the architect will make one final, detailed inspection. Errors and defects must then be corrected by the contractor. Once these matters are set right, the architect will recommend that the contractor be paid in full. Any later changes usually require the negotiation of a new contract and payment of a fee for service.

If there is a secret to trouble-free add-ons, it's clear communication between architects and clients. The thirty residential designs on the following pages directly express the client's special needs and desires. Each clearly expresses the direct line of communication that exists between the architect's expertise and the client's needs. Although the projects may appear relatively simple in form and execution, the final results were achieved through careful planning and the inventive use of materials and space. Home owners seeking to gain space, comfort, utility, and aesthetic enjoyment by constructing additions to their homes will find within these pages many imaginative design ideas and practical working methods that will move them closer to architect, drafting table, bank loan, and an imaginative add-on of their own.

1. Curved Sun Room Brightens Adobe Home

The reputation of designer Valerie Walsh as the builder of innovative solar greenhouses in the Southwest led the owners of a large ranch outside Santa Fe, New Mexico, to ask her to create a sun room at the southern end of their 1,000-square-foot living room. In addition to year-round space for plants and flowers, they wanted a sunny room that they described as "soft, with no hard lines" to conflict with the existing adobe architecture. Anything hard-edged, they told the designer, would look "tacked on."

So Walsh designed a 21-foot curved addition which would occupy a portion of a 20 x 40-foot flagstone patio *(below)*. Above the insulated, foot-thick adobe kneewall, she placed ten wood-framed casement windows and Lexan plastic sheets for overhead glazing. The roof of the addition was capped in copper. Fir rafters, which support the overhead glazing

12 and copper roof, are bolted into a steel plate that sits atop a massive interior post. The overhead glazing is embedded in a dry gasket system to keep water from entering the sun room. The vertical posts between the operating casement windows are framed in pine, but finished in mahogany for its ability to withstand weathering.

Inside the sun room the designer built a full adobe banco which the owners use primarily to hold their plants. In the base of the banco are recessed electric heaters. The interior wood trim throughout the addition is select pine, which Walsh stained and finished with a non-toxic sealant to protect the vegetation.

While the entire sun room addition was built for $7,000, Walsh says that the same project would cost considerably more today. Now, however, many builders around the country are experienced in working economically with large numbers of windows and overhead glazing. Appropriate products, finishes, and resources for such projects are readily available as well.

Interior of the south-facing addition contains a large banco in keeping with the adobe-style architecture throughout the house. Although planned for seating, the banco is seldom used by the owners for anything other than holding their plants.

Although the owners chose to remove two pairs of French doors from their living room after the sun room was built, Walsh recommends that there be a way to thermally separate a sun room from the rest of the house, since the addition loses heat at night and during winter months.

The roof structure of the addition is supported by a massive post placed at the entrance of the sun room. This post bears the weight of six fir rafters that are bolted into a steel plate at the top of the post.

The overhead glazing is composed of Lexan plastic sheets that are embedded in a dry gasket system located at all joints and under the copper roof at the hub of the rafters.

The rafters, post, and casement windows are trimmed in 1 x 4 and 2 x 6 select pine. This interior trim was stained and finished with a non-toxic sealant to protect the plants that fill the room.

The 21-foot arc of the sun room contains ten operating casement windows. These south-facing units sit atop an insulated, foot-thick adobe kneewall. Overhead, Lexan plastic sheets form the glazed roof.

The interior contains a full adobe banco, finished with wire lath and plaster, in keeping with the adobe architecture of the New Mexico ranch.

2. Oriel Brings Light and View to Victorian Dining Room

The owners of a large Victorian residence located in a small town in eastern Pennsylvania wanted an oriel, or bay window, added to a blank wall at the back of their house. They wanted more light and air, and a better view, but knew that such an add-on to a period house called for special care in the design, materials, and construction work. So they called in James and Elizabeth Facinelli, old-house specialists who manage a design and construction firm called Restorations Unlimited.

The actual window unit (shown on the following pages) is composed of three separate, double-hung wood windows. Such a bay window costs about $1,300 today and is readily available from local lumber yards. But it's not an easy task to install. Much work must precede its installation.

To start the job the Facinellis cut a hole in the rear wall of the house and installed a header, or heavy support studs, across the opening. They also cut through the floor, exposed the existing joists, and installed additional floor beams. At this point the Facinellis laid plywood sheets over the floor joists and framed in three short walls upon which the bay window unit would sit.

With the floor and stud walls in place, the oriel was installed. The owners had agreed to cover the oriel with a copper roof, which is both handsome and long-lasting. However, such a roof requires considerable time and patience to ensure the integrity of the flashing between the roof and the sidewall.

Once the roof was in place, the Facinellis could install insulation and plywood sheathing to the exterior. Since the original siding was wood, they installed the same graduated siding on the exterior, rather than aluminum or vinyl siding that would have destroyed the integrity of the late nineteenth-century house.

On the inside the Facinellis installed drywall on the stud walls and 2-inch oak flooring. They removed a short winding stair to the second floor and the small pantry closet it contained under its steps. As a final touch they added a Victorian railing salvaged from a demolished house to the stairs which reach the dining room from the basement.

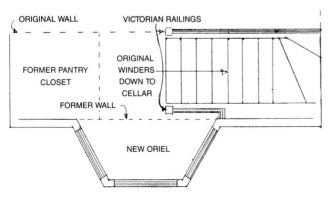

ORIGINAL WALL   VICTORIAN RAILINGS

FORMER PANTRY
CLOSET

ORIGINAL
WINDERS
DOWN TO
CELLAR

FORMER WALL

NEW ORIEL

The oriel, or bay window, addition (*opposite*) to this Victorian house in eastern Pennsylvania required the opening of the rear wall (*left, top*) to reveal the existing stud wall frame. Once these studs were removed, the opening was braced by additional wall supports and floor joists. The oriel was then installed (*left, center*). Note how well the new wood siding on the oriel addition matches the old clapboard on the existing wall.

The interior (*above*) of the oriel is composed of three double-hung wood windows which were joined in a common frame by a local lumberyard. Additional floor space gained by the add-on is minimal (*see plan*), yet it made a large difference to a small, dark room. The entire add-on project would cost about $4,500 today, including materials and the considerable labor involved.

3. Farmhouse Renovation Adds Studio and Greenhouse

When planning the addition of an architectural studio to his own home, architect Joe Hylton married his own desires and abilities with the pecularities of a small 1910 farmhouse in Norman, Oklahoma. He wanted the project to employ only wood and to include solar heating systems, preserve the character of the original structure, and allow him to perform all demolition and construction jobs except the electrical and plumbing work.

The long and narrow lot and local building codes dictated that the studio be added to the north side of the structure. Street access required that the main entrances to the studio and residence be located on the east. And the southern exposure of the structure enforced placement of a solar greenhouse on the front of the house.

The exterior incorporates several roof lines so that the 600-square-foot addition does not visually overpower the 690-square-foot residence. Instead of a conventional eight-foot ceiling in the studio, Hylton left the room open to the peak in the well-insulated roof. Off the studio entrance he built a cedar deck, complete with hot tub and a fence for privacy.

To tie together the old and new structures, Hylton salvaged and reused all of the original wood siding and trim. He gutted the interior, removed the old lath and plaster, insulated the walls, and drywalled all interior surfaces. The original wood floors were sanded and resealed. Even the claw feet of the original bathtub were cleaned and re-brassed.

The front porch was removed and replaced by a greenhouse. Bricks and an old concrete sidewalk provide heat storage and a seating area. Old radiators, which are filled with a mixture of ethylene-glycol and water, provide additional heat storage. Operable stained-glass windows, which open onto the greenhouse, allow plenty of light and natural ventilation in the living room. The handsome results of the architect's efforts may be seen on the following pages.

The original structure *(top)* was completely gutted by the owner, architect Joe Hylton, who also designed and built the studio addition to the small house. To preserve the character of the 1910 structure, the wood trim was salvaged and reused throughout the residence and studio.

Because of site limitations, building codes, and the size of the original structure, the studio was added to the north side of the residence *(at right in bottom photo).* Separate entrances to the residence and the studio ensure privacy in both areas.

The renovation project included the addition of a greenhouse on the south side of the living room. As well as providing space heating, the greenhouse provides room for plants and additional living space.

The original front porch was replaced by a greenhouse *(above)* which is reached through the master bedroom, living room, and its own entrance. Solar heat is stored in bricks stacked at the back of the greenhouse along the living room wall. Atop the bricks a recycled concrete sidewalk provides both seating and heat storage. Note the solar domestic hot water panels on the roof above the living room.

Radiators, salvaged from an old house, provide additional heat storage in the greenhouse *(left)* and are painted flat black to absorb the power of the sun's rays.

Since the greenhouse also provides a place for growing plants, the floor was constructed by laying three inches of hand-tamped sand and old sidewalk bricks, a building scheme that adds thermal storage mass and allows spilled water to drain.

Along the east side of the add-on is a multilevel cedar deck *(opposite)*. For added space, the deck planes are staggered and several irregular shapes are used to reach the hot tub. A sawtooth fence provides both privacy and the illusion of a much larger space.

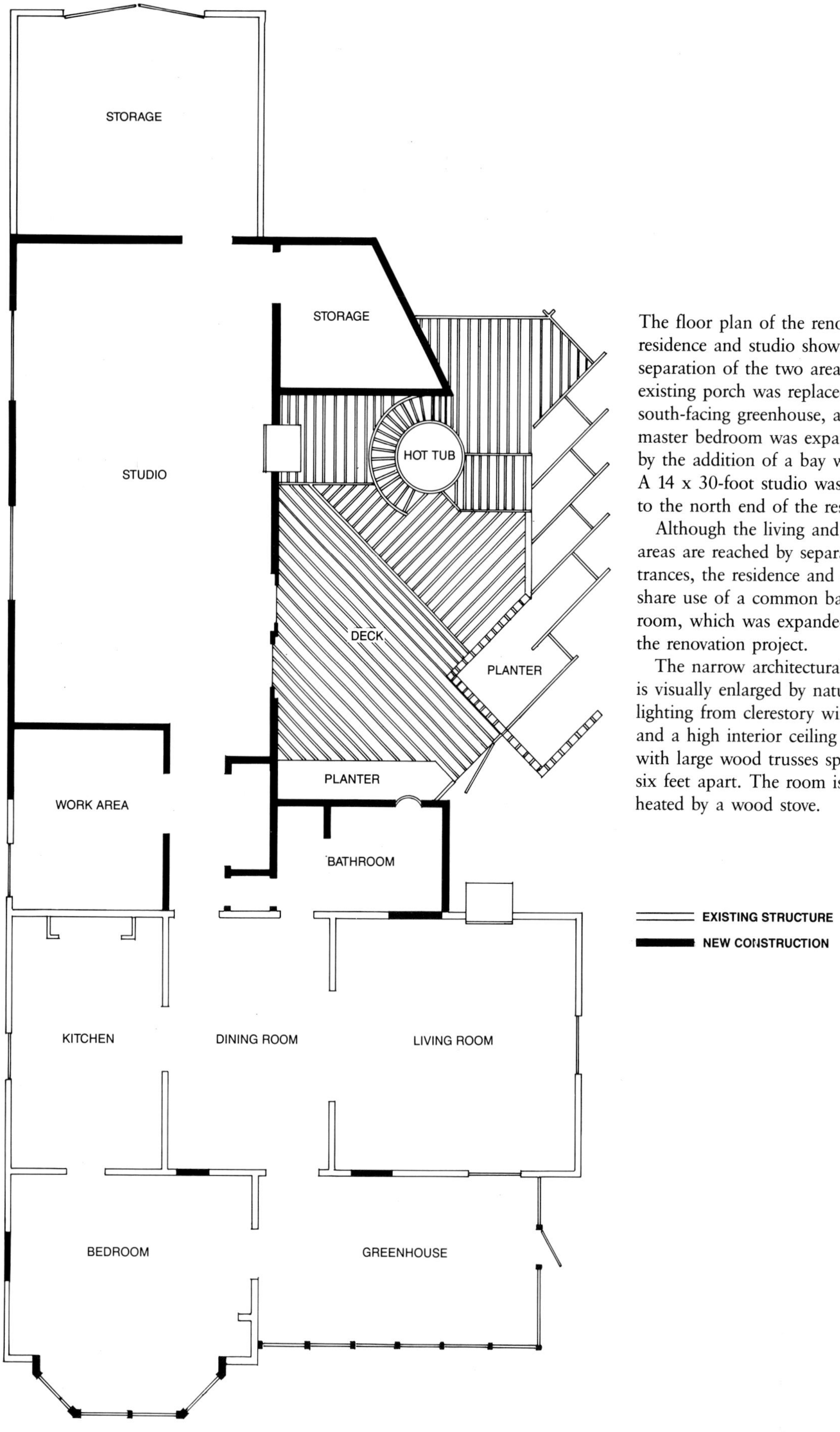

STORAGE

STORAGE

HOT TUB

STUDIO

DECK

PLANTER

WORK AREA

PLANTER

BATHROOM

The floor plan of the renovated residence and studio shows the separation of the two areas. The existing porch was replaced by a south-facing greenhouse, and the master bedroom was expanded by the addition of a bay window. A 14 x 30-foot studio was added to the north end of the residence.

Although the living and work areas are reached by separate entrances, the residence and studio share use of a common bathroom, which was expanded in the renovation project.

The narrow architectural studio is visually enlarged by natural lighting from clerestory windows and a high interior ceiling built with large wood trusses spaced six feet apart. The room is heated by a wood stove.

EXISTING STRUCTURE
NEW CONSTRUCTION

KITCHEN

DINING ROOM

LIVING ROOM

BEDROOM

GREENHOUSE

4. Seaside Space for Home Hobbyists

The seaside residence on the following pages has a history of additions and remodelings. Located on the eastern end of Long Island, New York, the original house was a 1950s ranch that was remodeled in the mid-1970s by architect Robert A.M. Stern. But the owners encountered financial difficulties during the construction project and sold the house to recover their investment. The new owners then hired architect Alfredo DeVido to complete the remodeling project and to design several additions to the front of the house.

The present owners, a middle-aged married couple, were nearing retirement and realized they wanted some serious space for their hobbies. (She is a gardener and he is a sculptor.) Once again they called on DeVido, who had also designed two office renovations for the husband's business. Ultimately, DeVido planned a greenhouse for her and a shop for him as well as additional room for house guests.

The owners didn't want the new wing to block their view of a nearby salt marsh pond and the Atlantic Ocean. So, instead of a tall, compact structure, the architect designed a long, low addition that lengthened the house along its east-west axis. At the far end of the new addition the greenhouse faces south for maximum sunlight. Although the resulting house is nearly twice as long as the existing structure, DeVido retained the same feeling throughout. Abundant windows, weathered shingles, and an unfettered circulation reinforce the open, sunlit atmosphere of the place.

Construction of the add-on took about six months. In the middle of the job the husband requested skylights over one of the galleries, even though the roof framing was already in place. This meant that the framing had to be ripped out, skylights ordered, and new framing installed. And instead of using inexpensive, stock Masonite pegboard for wall storage in the shop, the owner asked for ⅜-inch oak sheets which had to be custom-drilled to accept hanging hardware. These and other changes raised the final costs of the construction job, but allowed the owners to achieve their exact wishes. Overall, costs for this "his and her" add-on ran about $100 per square foot in what is obviously not a poor man's house.

To satisfy the leisure needs of his clients, architect Alfredo DeVido planned two separate spaces in one add-on. At the far end of the addition he built a greenhouse *(below)* for the wife. Stock wood windows form the hexagonal shape. The entire greenhouse, with its glass-topped roof, is bathed in sunlight the year 'round.

The greenhouse interior *(opposite)* has ample work space, storage, and display areas. What makes this space especially inviting for the wife is its separation from, yet proximity to, the husband's shop. Access to the greenhouse is afforded through a gallery near the husband's shop and from the yard.

Gliding patio doors, which split the greenhouse along its diameter, allow the outer half to be closed off from the rest of the add-on. In the winter this prevents the escape of heat and eliminates the need to heat the outer half of the structure.

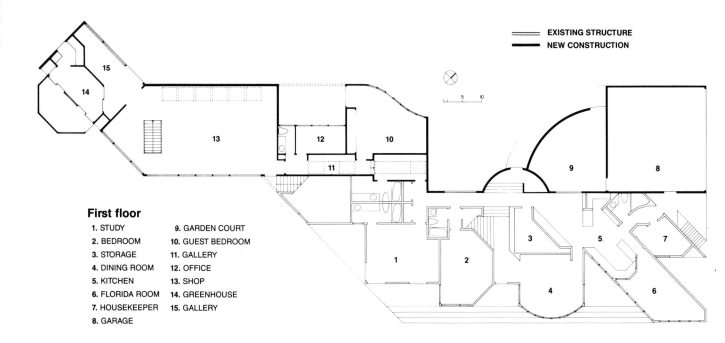

EXISTING STRUCTURE
NEW CONSTRUCTION

First floor

1. STUDY
2. BEDROOM
3. STORAGE
4. DINING ROOM
5. KITCHEN
6. FLORIDA ROOM
7. HOUSEKEEPER
8. GARAGE
9. GARDEN COURT
10. GUEST BEDROOM
11. GALLERY
12. OFFICE
13. SHOP
14. GREENHOUSE
15. GALLERY

Because the owners didn't want an addition that would block their ocean view, this "his and her" add-on is low and long *(see plan above)*.

The shingle-clad addition matches the existing structure *(opposite, top)* in both materials and feeling.

Although the husband's shop and the wife's greenhouse are highly individualized spaces, they both wanted as many windows as possible. This penchant for abundant natural lighting extends to the sculpture gallery *(below)*. Its steeply pitched roof is composed solely of north-facing windows.

The husband's shop *(opposite, bottom)* is also well-lit. In addition to windows on all walls, there are clerestories at the top of the room and skylights in the roof.

The architect gave the owners an add-on with much functional space for their money. Yet the owners' desire for natural lighting gave their addition a magic that money alone can't buy.

5. Guest House Matches Adobe-Style Home

In an old apple orchard along the Rio Grande Valley architect Robert Peters designed an energy-efficient guest house addition for the owner of an adobe home. Built in the traditional Pueblo style common to New Mexico, the 967-square-foot add-on contains a large family room with a south-facing greenhouse, a small bedroom, kitchen, and a bath. Located at the west end of the property, the addition includes a shaded patio that is favored with a clear view through rows of apple trees toward the distant Sandia Mountains in the east.

The greenhouse, an integral element of the structure, affords direct-gain solar heating. Six vertical, water-filled drums, which are painted heat-absorbing black on the exterior face and white on the interior, act as passive heat storage elements. A heat-circulating fireplace warms the family room, while a conventional gas-fired furnace and evaporative cooler provide back-up heating and cooling.

All window openings in the guest house are double-glazed units. Small casement windows in the family room and bedroom, plus air grills above the water drums in the greenhouse, provide natural ventilation. Roof windows in the bedroom and bath provide additional daylighting and winter heat gain to interior spaces.

A covered walkway, or portal, provides passage to the main house. A wood lattice screen on one side offers security from the street as it allows glimpses of the garden and orchard from the driveway.

From the main house, the guest house add-on is reached by a brick-paved walkway, or portal *(right)*, in the adobe style common to New Mexico. The wood lattice screen shields the street-side view, yet allows glimpses of the apple orchard from the driveway.

The family room *(below)* contains both living and dining areas. Additional space is provided by the "banco" seating, located on either side of the fireplace, which opens up as twin beds for children.

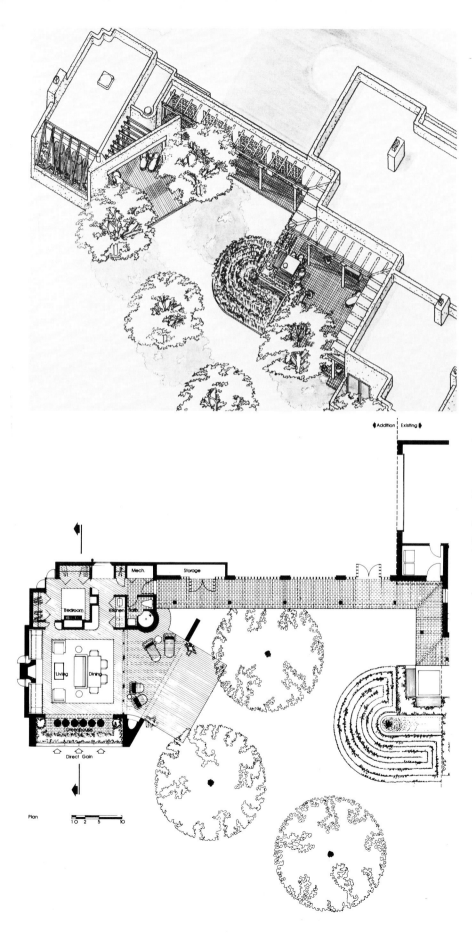

Plan

Addition | Existing

Mech. | Storage

Bedroom

Kitchen | Bath

Living | Dining

Greenhouse

Direct Gain

10 2 5   10

Built to match the traditional Pueblo style of the main house, the guest house addition is reached by a covered walkway. As the plan *(left, top)* shows, wood louvers over the patio are angled to provide summertime shading, yet admit low winter sun.

The addition provides a large room for entertaining and use as a family room, a small bedroom, a kitchen unit, and a bath. The plan of the guest house provides a winter focus toward the heat-circulating fireplace in the living room area. During the summer the focus shifts to the outdoor deck, which is reached by sliding patio doors off the dining area. The cost of the 967-square-foot addition, which was completed in 1980, was about $71,000. By moving guests into separate quarters, the owners were able to remodel their existing residence to gain additional bedroom space for their children.

6. A New Angle on Suburban Living

Tract houses are an affordable choice for many Americans. But the numbing repetition of their exterior designs and their boxy floor plans leave much to be desired. Fortunately, adding on offers home owners a chance to gain new living space and to improve the appearance of their suburban properties. Such was the case for the owners of a bi-level house near Cincinnati. They wanted an add-on that would complement the design and materials of their twelve-year-old structure. But they wanted it to stand on its own as an attractive new element.

Specifically, architect Stan Better was asked to expand a lower level family room, expose a view of the back yard and pool, create a new link to the living room on the second floor, and reshape the adjoining kitchen. He was also asked to limit the construction cost to $35,000.

By angling the two-story addition to ensure passive solar heating, Better built an add-on that strikes a note of individuality in the neighborhood. His design strategy also focused the view toward the owner-built pool and deck as well as a nearby ravine and woods. Although the addition contains 250 square feet of actual floor space, it feels as if a much larger area has been added to the house.

Since the architect's remodeling company built the add-on, he was able to obtain economical building materials for the windows, doors, walls, and siding. Most of the cabinets were retained in the remodeled kitchen, which now includes an eating counter that overlooks the add-on. And even though the owners wanted an expensive spiral staircase and a quarry-tile floor, Better completed the four-month renovation and addition project considerably under budget!

In the expanded family room, the view stretches toward the back yard. A large portion of the existing room (foreground) contains the same quarry-tile flooring as the addition. This further expands the 250-square-foot space while it joins the add-on to the existing house.

Sunlight reaches the back of the family room through the window walls, skylights, and upper-story windows of the add-on. A spiral staircase links the family room on the lower level to the living room, dining area, and renovated kitchen on the second floor.

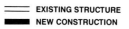

EXISTING STRUCTURE
NEW CONSTRUCTION

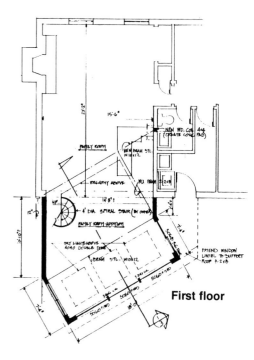

First floor

The two-story addition was built atop a concrete patio previously installed by the owner. The sequence of construction photographs *(left, top to bottom)* shows how the family room addition was nearly completed before the adjoining wall was opened. Once the addition was closed in, the patio door on the lower level and the living room window on the second floor were removed.

Construction began by joining a 2 x 6 stud wall, 10 feet long, to the existing structure. The first floor walls of the add-on were then angled south, toward the pool. The second-story windows were supported by a steel beam which crosses the newly-created space. Since the addition captures so much solar heat, the ceilings were insulated with nine inches of fiberglass batts.

In the floor plans *(above)* the add-on appears as a rectangular

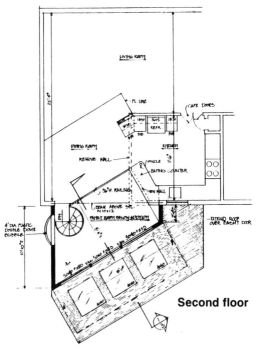

Second floor

room that abuts the existing house at a 45-degree angle. While ensuring passive solar heating, the angled addition breaks up the boxy appearance of the suburban house. Note how the spiral staircase allows easy access between the expanded family room on the lower level and the living room on the second floor.

The completed add-on *(right, top)* shows the skylights above the family room seating area. The angled addition orients the focus of the room toward the pool and back yard. The addition was finished to match the exterior of the existing structure.

The remodeled kitchen now includes an eating counter. Sitting at this counter, the view *(right, bottom)* into the add-on includes a four-foot-diameter plastic dome window and the connecting spiral staircase along the western wall, dramatic fare for any casual meal.

The dramatic transformation of
this bi-level suburban home from
the monotonous design of tract
housing to an architectural statement of efficiency and individuality clearly demonstrates the ex-
citing potentiality of carefully
planned, cost-effective add-ons.

7. / Greenhouse Brightens City House Interiors

Additions to houses on narrow city lots pose special problems. Often they can be placed only at the top or rear of the structure. But an add-on that makes a building taller necessitates extra stairs or structural support, while an add-on that makes the building longer means the interior may be dark. So, when renovating a brownstone on a 17-foot-wide lot, architect Frank Caminiti of Architrave, a New York City firm, added a two-story greenhouse *(below)* to the rear of the building. This brought sunlight into the kitchen on the first floor and into the full depth of the living room on the second floor, and made the entire structure feel larger.

The greenhouse was added to the south end of a 2,450-square-foot renovation project designed *(basement plan below)* by the New York architectural firm Architrave. Before purchasing the building, the owner and the architect visited several structures. Each building was inspected with an eye on the feasibility and cost of the renovation project envisioned by the owner.

The selected building, which contained extensive damage to the interior, was purchased for $117,000. The original renovation budget of $200,000 included several structural changes, wall bracing, a new heating system, and a renovated full basement. However, the owner exceeded this figure by about $50,000 when he requested numerous luxury finishes and materials during the middle of the construction project.

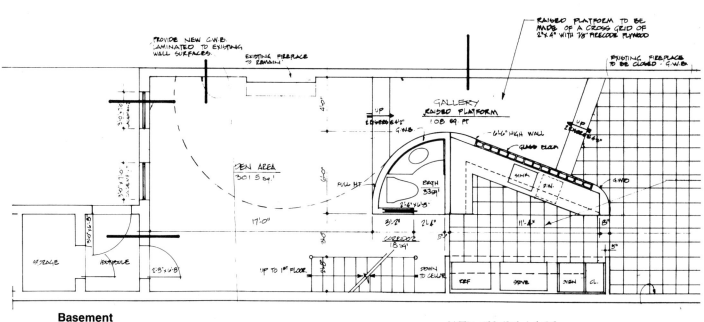

Basement

Before the renovation, the rear wall of the brownstone structure was simply a masonry wall with two windows on each level. These were removed and two eight-inch steel channels were inserted to reinforce the building's frame. This allowed two large openings at the rear of the building where the greenhouse was added.

The lower level of the greenhouse *(opposite, top)* opens into the dining area and kitchen of the renovated structure. Four sliding aluminum doors, which move along tracks located in the floor and ceiling, can be stored in a wall pocket behind the circular stair. This steel-framed unit, only six feet in diameter, reduced the amount of floor space in the greenhouse that would have been required for a more formal staircase.

On the second-floor landing *(above),* three pairs of custom-made mahogany doors open into the living room. The slanted portion of the greenhouse contains electrically-operated mechanical blinds which are adjustable to any angle and control the amount of sunlight entering the greenhouse and living areas of the house. All windows and doors are double-glazed tempered glass.

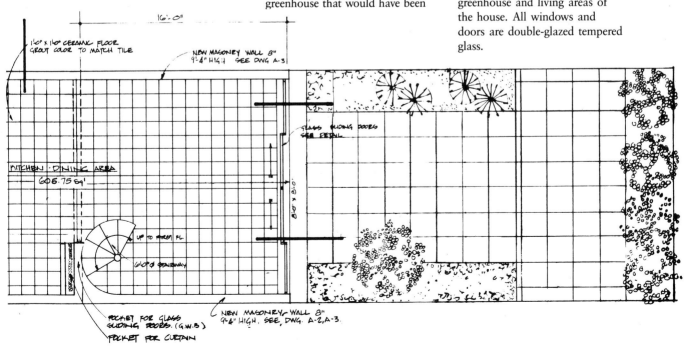

8. A Sunny Addition for Family Entertaining

A love of square-dancing led to the large, sunny room addition shown here. In their quest for space in which to entertain, the owners of this suburban New Jersey house found that the south side was the most obvious location for an add-on. It contained only three small windows and was heavily shaded by nearby deciduous trees. These fortuitous circumstances

The 200-square-foot sun space, attached to the south side of the house, is reached through the playroom on the first floor and the living room on the second floor. The existing brick chimney and 12 x 12-inch slate flooring act as heat storage media.

enabled architect Grayson Ferrante of the Princeton Energy Group to plan a 200-square-foot addition that employed passive solar concepts.

During extreme temperature variations, a sun space of this type is usually shut off from the rest of the house by a door or window. Energy calculations made before construction, however, showed that trees eliminated most of the summer sun's heat gain, while thermal curtains across the south-facing window wall and in the slanted roof would prevent night-time heat loss during the winter. Overall, the energy calculation determined that the sun space would gain more heat annually than it lost even if it was left open to the rest of the house.

While the sun space was initially planned as an extra space for entertainment, the family uses it for many day-to-day activities. And, as a result of the add-on, natural daylight has been introduced to the most used areas of the house.

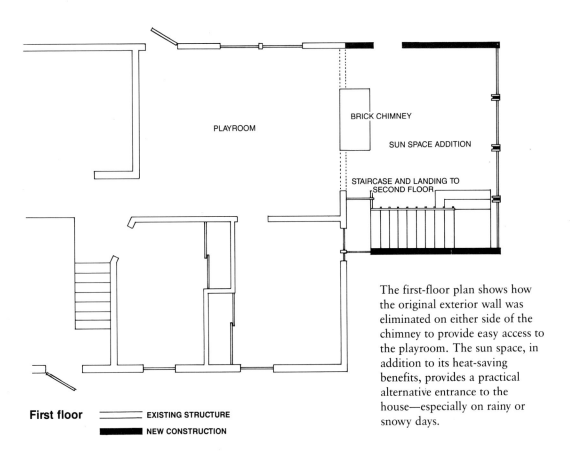

PLAYROOM

BRICK CHIMNEY

SUN SPACE ADDITION

STAIRCASE AND LANDING TO SECOND FLOOR

First floor   ======= EXISTING STRUCTURE
                  ▬▬▬▬▬▬▬ NEW CONSTRUCTION

The first-floor plan shows how the original exterior wall was eliminated on either side of the chimney to provide easy access to the playroom. The sun space, in addition to its heat-saving benefits, provides a practical alternative entrance to the house—especially on rainy or snowy days.

Surrounded by many deciduous trees, the sun space is shaded during summer and sun-filled during winter.

The south-facing window wall and slanted roof *(left)* contain thermal curtains which control nighttime heat loss during winter. Because the owners of passive solar houses must remember to open and close such curtains, it is often said that such homes are designed for active people. This sun space design, however, reduces such activities to a minimum.

9. Oak-trimmed Addition Replaces Austere Kitchen

Dull, uninviting spaces need ornament or detail to whet our visual appetites. When a kitchen—the most lived-in room of a house—is both unattractive and cramped, then it's time to call in an architect to create additional space with warmth and character.

Such was the case for this add-on project in Piedmont, California. The simple addition of six feet of floor space and four feet of outdoor deck around the corner of an existing kitchen and breakfast room afforded architect Glen Jarvis an opportunity to improve a very plain house substantially.

Inside, Jarvis expanded the kitchen and created a new dining area. The existing dining room was converted into a den. The newly-planned kitchen, trimmed throughout in oak, has as its central feature a butcher block-topped island counter. The tidy work triangle is not hindered by the flow of traffic, yet the cook can converse with guests and family in the dining area or enjoy a view toward the sunny back yard.

Another highlight of this new kitchen is the 24-foot storage wall, which is paneled in oak. By combining the broom closet, refrigerator, pantry, laundry, and other storage closets in one place, the architect eliminated clutter and formalized the appearance of this inviting room.

On the exterior, the wraparound deck joins the house with its heretofore lackluster yard. French doors on each side of the dining area admit sunlight and passing breezes to the revitalized home.

Before it was added to, this small West Coast house lacked not only charm and grace, but sufficient kitchen work space and room for seating. A stucco-clad box, the exterior lacked detail and character.

The addition of six feet of floor space and four feet of deck around the south corner of the house allowed the enterprising architect to expand the kitchen and dining areas. He added a tile roof, French doors, and a landscaped deck, which enliven the back yard and add a distinctly Spanish-Colonial flavor, suitable for this part of the country *(top)*.

The cook's view of the dining and seating area *(center)* includes the deck and sunny yard. Jarvis allowed the ceiling in the addition to reach the full height of the new roof. The oak-trimmed French doors and hand-adzed beams add warmth and personality to the add-on interior.

Opposite the sink and the delightful antique stove, which was rescued from the original kitchen, the butcher block counter provides ample work space in the new kitchen *(bottom)*. Wood casement windows are trimmed in oak to match all cabinetry and doors.

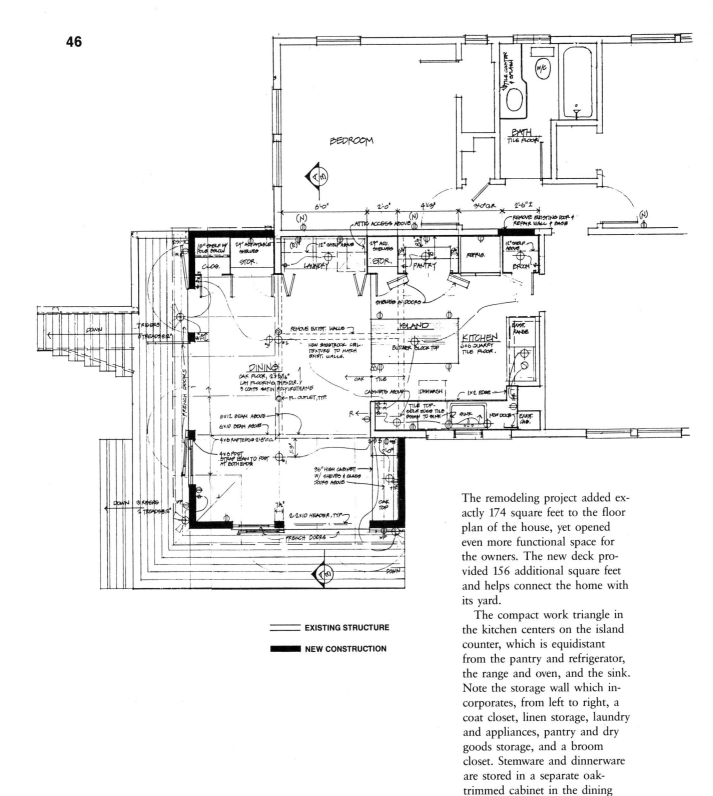

EXISTING STRUCTURE

NEW CONSTRUCTION

The remodeling project added exactly 174 square feet to the floor plan of the house, yet opened even more functional space for the owners. The new deck provided 156 additional square feet and helps connect the home with its yard.

The compact work triangle in the kitchen centers on the island counter, which is equidistant from the pantry and refrigerator, the range and oven, and the sink. Note the storage wall which incorporates, from left to right, a coat closet, linen storage, laundry and appliances, pantry and dry goods storage, and a broom closet. Stemware and dinnerware are stored in a separate oak-trimmed cabinet in the dining area.

The view from the south corner of the kitchen and breakfast room *(above)* before the renovation project shows just how cramped and constricted the space was before the rooms were opened up and added to. For dramatic comparison, note the view from the kitchen *(right, top)* after the renovation. From this position the cook can now see guests and family in the dining area and beyond into the back yard. The sense of added space is far greater than the actual square feet provided by the architect.

Oak doors on the storage wall *(right, bottom)* add not only a formal, uncluttered appearance to the entire kitchen but suggest the richness of a fully-paneled wall that unites both kitchen and dining room.

47

10. Facilities Expanded for Efficient Entertaining

What do you do if you're cramped for space and can't literally add on additional room for one reason or another? Why, you do what a West Coast couple did when they wanted to enlarge their kitchen: you "add on" space by "borrowing" it from an adjacent area of the house.

Because they entertain frequently, the couple was in need of a kitchen that was both spacious and efficient. The original room was considerably large to begin with, but more space had been allotted to an eat-in dining area than to the kitchen facilities themselves. What's more, the limited work space lacked adequate storage and clean-up room. To handle the muss and fuss required for dinner parties of eighteen or twenty guests, the couple needed an open plan that separated work space from storage areas. They also wanted an efficient layout that would allow four people to cook, serve, and clean at the same time.

Donald Silvers, a Los Angeles kitchen consultant and chef, redesigned the kitchen by relocating the major elements. He completely removed the eat-in dining area and stole usable space from a laundry closet. In the new plan, he included a U-shaped work center in what was the former eating area and a separate clean-up and dish storage area in the former galley kitchen. To gain additional wall space for cabinets, he closed off a door to the dining room and expanded a second entry.

In the food preparation area, traffic moves in one continuous line: from the refrigerator to the sink and tiled countertop, then on to the grill, cooktop, and ovens. Prepared dishes are then served to guests in the dining room or are passed through a window to a service counter near the family's swimming pool.

What makes this particular kitchen so efficient is its separate clean-up area, an amenity that allows several kitchen hands to work at the same time without getting under foot. Here the designer has installed a double sink and dishwasher as well as spacious storage space for dinnerware.

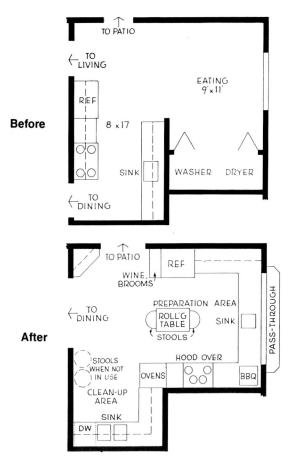

Before

TO PATIO

TO LIVING

EATING
9' x 11'

REF

8 x 17

SINK   WASHER   DRYER

TO DINING

After

TO PATIO

WINE, BROOMS

REF

TO DINING

PREPARATION AREA

ROLL'G TABLE

SINK

STOOLS

PASS-THROUGH

STOOLS WHEN NOT IN USE

HOOD OVER

CLEAN-UP AREA

OVENS

BBQ

SINK

DW

Traffic moved through the middle of the work area in the old kitchen *("before" plan)* and too much space was given to the eating area. The designer removed several walls and relocated the washer and dryer units, thereby opening additional work space in the new kitchen.

In the expanded room *("after" plan)* the food preparation area is separated from the clean-up area. In lieu of an island counter, the owners use a rolling table. Depending on its location, the table serves as a temporary work area, snack counter, room divider, or clean-up caddy.

The key to efficiency in the new kitchen *(below)* is the proximity and the separation of the food preparation and clean-up areas. Both work stations contain their own sinks as well as generous amounts of oak cabinets and counter space.

The food preparation area of the expanded kitchen *(above)* is a model of efficient work space. Traffic flows from the refrigerator or oak pantry cabinets to the sink, appliances, and countertop; it then moves to the grill, cooktop, or ovens; and then on to the diners in the dining room or on the patio. A pass-through window over the sink speeds the delivery or return of dishes from the patio.

The rolling table adjoins a counter whenever it is needed, creating a peninsula for additional work space and channeling the flow of traffic out of the cook's way. With stools in place, the rolling table serves as a convenient dining table for informal meals.

11. Kitchen Expansion Updates Town House

In the days when servants were affordable and readily available, meals were prepared in the basement of this Federal-era town house in Philadelphia. A pantry on the first floor served as a convenient way station to the formal dining room. In the servantless 1980s, however, it is only practical to prepare and serve meals on the same floor. Having made use of a narrow servant's pantry as a temporary kitchen for as long as they could, the present-day owners of this historic property challenged architect Jim Kruhly to adapt and add on to this space sufficient room for cooking, storage, clean-up, and informal dining. The dramatic result is pictured below.

52 The floor plan *(below)* illustrates how the kitchen and dining area were added on to the rear of the existing house, at a right angle incorporating a portion of what was once a bleak back yard on a typical nineteenth-century Philadelphia alley. Because of the narrow width of the available kitchen space, two sets of counters were installed. Along the party wall a standard 25-inch counter for food preparation, sink, and range is used. Opposite this is the exterior wall which contains an 18-inch-wide counter used primarily for temporary placement of utensils, dinnerware, and grocery sacks. The most surprising element of the add-on is the semicircular breakfast nook. Because the space is formed in part by a curved wall, there is an illusion of spaciousness, even though the curve extends the room by only two feet. Allowance has been made for a buffet counter and a storage cabinet, as well as a place for cookbooks.

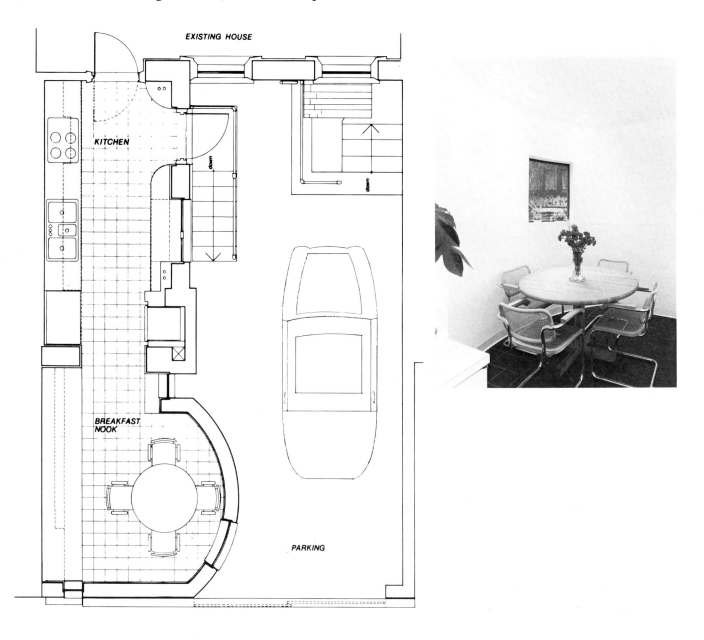

Since the property is only 22 feet wide, space for the add-on was available at a premium. The "before" and "after" views *(left)* of the addition's exterior show how neatly the resourceful architect used the back yard's space. Windows were strategically located to bring in light and to control the view. Even as he snared space for the breakfast nook, the designer retained space for the owner's automobile.

Before the addition, the owners had used a cramped servant's pantry *(right)* as their kitchen. This space was grossly inadequate for preparing and serving meals. The add-on to the pantry is not wider than the original space, but is considerably longer. The proper placement of counters and cabinets has created a highly efficient work area and added an unobtrusive touch of modernity to an otherwise traditional nineteenth-century town house.

12. "Bump Out" Forms Cook's New Space

The need for more room in a kitchen is usually felt by the person who spends the most time and labor there. As soon as the owners of this house in California, a couple with three children, decided they needed more kitchen storage and seating space, the wife began a list of every culinary item they possessed. By the time architect Jacob Sofer of the Architectural Design Group in Palo Alto arrived, she had a ten-page list of pots and pans, appliances, dinnerware, silverware, and utensils. She asked the architect to replan the kitchen in her fifty-year-old house so there would be enough room for everything on her list plus her family and guests.

Sofer was also given a list of specific functions and work spaces that must be incorporated in the design of the new kitchen. These included a baking garage (a small cabinet for storing

a mixer and its accessories) and countertop work space near the ovens; a sink near the enlarged windows that overlook the back yard; a cooktop near the seating area, so the cook could converse with family and guests without interrupting her work; butcher block countertops for food preparation near the cooktop; and even a pull-out shelf for the TV in a wall cabinet, so it could be viewed from both the kitchen and seating area.

At first the project appeared to call for a simple reworking of the floor plan, appliance layout, storage areas, and traffic pattern. But when the architect couldn't make room for all the storage space his client wanted, he removed a door in the eat-in dining area and added a 3-foot-wide "bump out" along a 16-foot section of exterior wall *(opposite)*. This relatively small addition under an existing eave opened enough space to replan the kitchen storage according to the cook's requirements. It also allowed Sofer to plan banquette seating in the eat-in area. The "bump-out" was fitted with two large fixed-pane windows and a pair of operating casements at each end of the newly formed bay. Flooded with morning sunlight, the kitchen now has a place for everything and everything in its place.

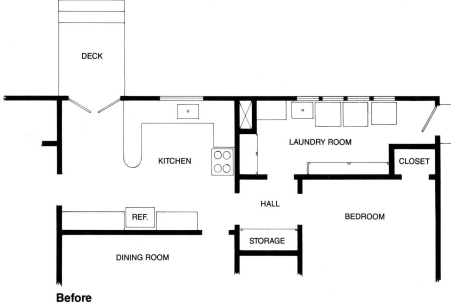

Before

After

Before renovation *(left)*, the California kitchen had inadequate storage and seating space for a growing family of five. So architect Jacob Sofer removed an exit door from the eat-in dining area and added a 3-foot-wide bay along the exterior wall of the kitchen.

The new plan *(left, bottom)*is split into two efficient areas: the cook's U-shaped work center and an eat-in dining area with banquette seating under the windows.

The new plan puts the sink, cooktop, and countertop work space in compact proximity. Additional pantry storage is provided next to the refrigerator and behind the louvered doors in the hall. In addition to banquette seating in the dining area, the "bump out" opened enough space for a TV, desk, and display case.

The renovation project also includes a new deck outside the kitchen and dining area, reached by a door off the laundry room.

13. Making Room for More Than One Cook

The owners of the Minnesota kitchen shown on the following pages entertain frequently in their back-yard patio, a landscaped space which includes a swimming pool and barbeque. Their outdoor facilities could accommodate a big crowd, but they lacked sufficient space when bad weather and colder seasons forced the party indoors.

Their old kitchen was small and dark, and lacked sufficient storage space. The appliances were inadequate for the family and its guests. So they asked Jim Krengel, the proprietor of Kitchens By Krengel in St. Paul, to increase the size of the kitchen, particularly the dining area. They wanted a kitchen that could accommodate more than one cook and make entertaining easy. They also wanted lots of windows and easy access to the patio and pool.

Krengel began by adding ten feet to the rear of the house. Then he divided the new kitchen into two separate areas, one for food preparation and one for entertaining. Each contains its own storage area, sink, and dishwasher.

The major element in the kitchen is an L-shaped center island. It contains a large expanse of countertop which separates the food preparation zone and the expanded dining area. At one end of the L is the primary work center, containing a refrigerator, sink, and cooktop. At the other end are the pantry, freezer, and ovens—a secondary work center. Finally, at the base of the L is the entertainment work center with its own sink, ice maker, dishwasher, and storage area.

The remodeled kitchen serves two separate functions: food storage and preparation *(above)* and dining, entertaining, and clean-up *(opposite)*. Each work area contains its own sink, disposer, and dishwasher. The food preparation area contains a cooktop and microwave and conventional ovens, while the dining area contains its own ice maker.

The L-shaped counter area, which separates traffic in both work centers, is a large expanse of plastic laminate with rectangles of contrasting color applied to the surfaces to reduce the counter's impact on the design scheme.

When the designer added ten feet to the rear of the existing kitchen, he also changed the roof line from a straight gable to two opposing gables. This allowed him to increase the 8-foot ceiling to a vaulted 12-foot height. This new shape made possible the in-

stallation of a trapezoid-shaped
window at the gable end of the
kitchen. This admits additional
natural illumination, which the
owners requested.

The kitchen cabinets match the
tile backsplash, rustic brick
hearth, and ceiling beams. Unlike
many kitchens that rely on stark
white finishes for a spare look,
this traditionally-styled space is
both homey and uncluttered.

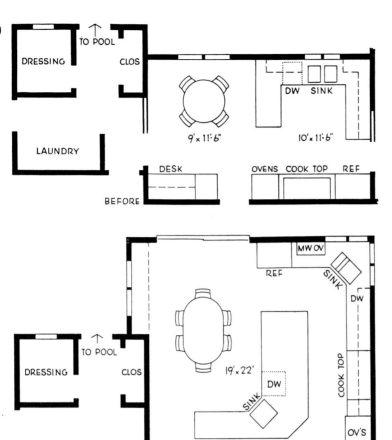

DRESSING TO POOL CLOS

LAUNDRY

9' × 11'-6"   DW   SINK   10' × 11'-6"

DESK   OVENS COOK TOP   REF

BEFORE

MW OV

REF   SINK

DW

COOK TOP

19' × 22'   DW

SINK

OV'S

DRESSING TO POOL CLOS

LAUNDRY

DESK   FRZR PANTRY

AFTER

As these "before" and "after" floor plans clearly show, the addition of only ten feet (and the professional services of a certified kitchen designer) has transformed a once-dark and crowded space into a seemingly palatial kitchen.

The major feature of the expanded kitchen is an L-shaped center island. It contains a large countertop that separates the food preparation and dining areas. At one end of the room is the primary work center, which contains a refrigerator, sink, disposer, dishwasher, cooktop, and microwave oven. In the other end is the entertainment work center with its own sink, ice maker, dishwasher, and storage cabinets.

Designed to serve a large family, the new kitchen features a large cooktop *(left)* and a pair of ovens. Surrounding this area are matching rustic brick, tile, and hickory wood cabinets.

14. Gazebo Inspires New Breakfast Room

When the owners of a 7,000-square foot house in northern California decided to remodel it, they called on Berkeley architect Glen Jarvis. They had seen other renovations by Jarvis that they liked and received favorable responses from all the references he supplied. They wanted the architect to help them restore the charm of their home, which was originally built in 1869 but had suffered the loss of many of its Victorian features over the years.

As an initial project, they invited Jarvis to design a breakfast room addition which would be located directly off the kitchen. The owners supplied the architect with a small sketch of their own ideas for the add-on. Not surprisingly, he felt that these plans could be improved, since Victorian structures employ various geometric shapes which can be readily added. Inspired by neighboring Victorian homes and a small gazebo in the owners' garden, he designed the 12-foot octagonal breakfast room shown on the following pages. Sitting in this new wing, the owners enjoy a prominent view of the main garden on the eastern end of their property.

The breakfast room addition *(overleaf)* and the adjacent kitchen (which was also remodeled) are nearly the same height—11 feet. The large window frames and paneled ceiling make the new room feel even larger than its actual dimensions. Although there is a large window area, the addition is well-insulated and weatherstripped, and uses double-glazed units. The room is bathed each day in morning sunlight. During the summer and most afternoons the exterior is shaded by deciduous vines. There is even a small arbor between the tall windows for additional shading. With all its windows and natural lighting, the breakfast room is used very much like an outdoor patio. In fact, because of its white-painted latticework and paneling, the add-on looks like a porch, original to the house, that had been enclosed sometime in the past.

Overleaf: The new breakfast room (seen from the remodeled kitchen). The exterior of the add-on, suggested by the gazebo in the owners' garden, reflects the other Queen Anne structures in the Victorian neighborhood.

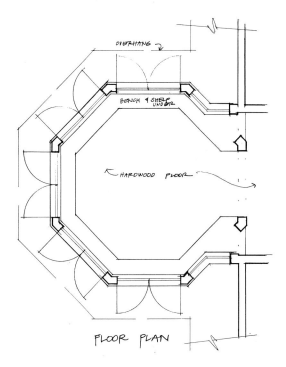

OVERHANG

BENCH & SHELF UNDER

← HARDWOOD FLOOR →

FLOOR PLAN

As the floor plan *(top)* shows, the 12-foot-wide breakfast room includes a bench for plants and shelf space for cookbooks along the interior wall. A random-width oak floor extends from the kitchen into the breakfast room. Five pairs of operating casement windows are shaded by an overhang.

Before the breakfast room was added *(center),* the eastern wall of the kitchen contained six fixed windows, which overlooked the main garden. Earlier renovations had removed the second story of the house and dramatically altered the appearance of the Victorian structure.

With the addition *(bottom)* of the breakfast room, the owners began the restoration of Victorian period elements to their home. The latticework, cross bars, and paneling of the octagonal add-on were also employed on the entry porch of the strucure. The kitchen was remodeled, a maid's room was converted into a family room, and the second story was restored to the structure.

Once work on the add-on began, it became clear that the owners wanted many quality materials and details, which increased the cost. The entire kitchen and remodeling project cost about $100,000, while the breakfast room cost about $20,000.

15. Relocated Entry Invites New Look at Old House

When architect Stephen Lasar set out to renovate an old Cape Cod-style house in western Connecticut, the task before him was clear. The owners of the house had asked him to expand a small and stuffy master bedroom suite, to introduce passive solar heating into two areas of the house, and to create a new entry in place of the existing one that was hidden from general view by the garage. In the process of fulfilling his client's requests, the architect succeeded in adding new warmth to an old house.

His first step was to move the front door from its location behind the garage to the wall of a passageway near the living room. This made the entry visible from the driveway. The old entrance was converted into a sun-filled plant room, to which was added a sitting area with a balcony. Skylights were installed in the sitting room roof to bring solar heat to this part of the house.

Next the architect removed the gypsum-board walls surrounding an existing fireplace that stood between the living room and the new entrance area. The exposed brick and the wider passageway imparted an open feeling to both the living room and the new entry.

Lasar then added a curved projection to the enlarged master bedroom in order to expand its floor space. This step created an inviting U-shaped courtyard in front of the new entry. The south-facing, double-hung windows in the bedroom were replaced with a wall of large fixed-pane windows to admit sunlight and solar heat. Insulated thermal shades reduce nighttime heat loss through these windows.

As a final touch Lasar remodeled the face of the garage and removed an overgrown trellis that stood opposite the master bedroom. With this step he opened a full view of the new entry from the driveway.

The new entry *(above)* to a large house in western Connecticut is clearly visible from the driveway and garage at right. The small courtyard, flagstone path, and sunlit front door make the entryway particularly inviting. The curved projecting wall at left softens the edge of the expanded master bedroom.

66

The south-facing wall of the master bedroom *(opposite, top)* is composed of five fixed-pane windows, each the size of patio doors. Solar heat gained through these windows and the skylight above them is stored in the tile floor. Insulated thermal curtains are used to reduce nighttime heat loss through the large glazing areas.

When the architect moved the entry, he converted the existing vestibule into a small plant room *(opposite, bottom)*. Large fixed-pane windows and a full-sized glass door admit sunlight and solar heat which, as in the bedroom, is stored in the tile floor. A small, narrow stairway leads to a loft above. It contains a skylight in the roof for additional solar gain in what had once been a dark, cold area of the house.

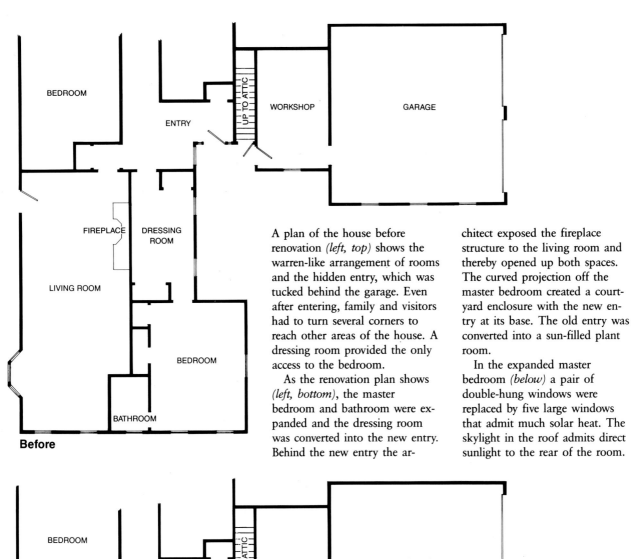

BEDROOM

ENTRY

UP TO ATTIC

WORKSHOP

GARAGE

FIREPLACE

DRESSING ROOM

LIVING ROOM

BEDROOM

BATHROOM

Before

A plan of the house before renovation *(left, top)* shows the warren-like arrangement of rooms and the hidden entry, which was tucked behind the garage. Even after entering, family and visitors had to turn several corners to reach other areas of the house. A dressing room provided the only access to the bedroom.

As the renovation plan shows *(left, bottom)*, the master bedroom and bathroom were expanded and the dressing room was converted into the new entry. Behind the new entry the ar-

chitect exposed the fireplace structure to the living room and thereby opened up both spaces. The curved projection off the master bedroom created a court-yard enclosure with the new entry at its base. The old entry was converted into a sun-filled plant room.

In the expanded master bedroom *(below)* a pair of double-hung windows were replaced by five large windows that admit much solar heat. The skylight in the roof admits direct sunlight to the rear of the room.

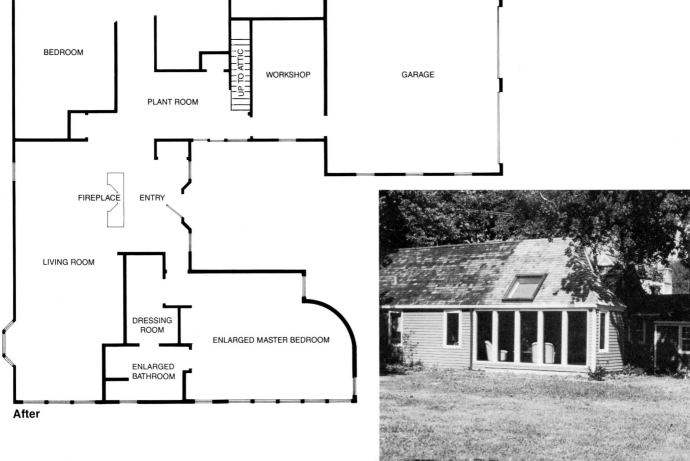

BEDROOM

PLANT ROOM

UP TO ATTIC

WORKSHOP

GARAGE

FIREPLACE

ENTRY

LIVING ROOM

DRESSING ROOM

ENLARGED MASTER BEDROOM

ENLARGED BATHROOM

After

16. Summer Bungalow Raised to New Heights

An older couple with four grown children wanted to add two rooms to their summer home, a 20 x 40-foot bungalow they built on Cape Cod in the early 1950s. But while the project was being discussed with architect Jim Kruhly, the size of the job expanded to include a major addition and modernization. Specifically, the couple wanted a basement, garage, family room, master bedroom, two bathrooms, a larger kitchen, and additional deck space. What's more, they wanted the addition to have a view of a nearby pond and not to overwhelm the character of the original structure.

To fill this tall list of requirements, Kruhly devised a crescent-shaped addition that is connected to the bungalow by a vestibule and large redwood deck. The new wing contains a family room over the garage and the master bedroom suite. The existing structure was lifted off its original block foundation to make room for the basement and rotated fifteen degrees for a better view of the pond. Inside, the kitchen and bath were renovated. Red cedar shingles and white trim cover the exterior of both structures.

The owners had a $60,000 budget for this project, but the overall cost reached $90,000 because they asked for many improvements and such deferred maintenance jobs as patching the roof and replacing the furnace. Unlike some projects with such cost overruns, the owners, architect, and contractor made these changes and improvements with few disagreements. The happy owners now have a large new home with increased circulation, and not merely two additional rooms.

The existing bungalow *(left)* was raised off its original block foundation *(right)* and supported on cribbing while the contractor built an 8-inch concrete-wall basement underneath. During the process the entire structure was slightly rotated to enable a better view of a nearby pond.

Because the owners loved their vacation house, a small and simple structure, they wanted the addition to be compatible yet interesting. Consequently, the architect planned a vertical add-on *(left)* for the existing horizontal structure.

The curving plan *(above)* affords a view past the main house toward a nearby pond. Connecting both structures are an entry vestibule and a large redwood deck that faces west.

EXIST. SCREENED PORCH

EXIST. LIVING ROOM

EXIST. STUDY

EXIST. BEDROOM

EXIST. DINING

KITCHEN

BATH 1

DECK

FAMILY ROOM

BATH 2

MASTER BEDROOM

EXISTING STRUCTURE

NEW CONSTRUCTION

The process of transforming a small summer bungalow into a year-round home on Cape Cod included raising and inserting a basement beneath it. A two-story addition with garage was attached to the main house by a connecting vestibule and a large deck. The addition contains a family room with vaulted ceiling and the master bedroom suite. Red cedar shingles and white trim maintain a uniform exterior.

17. Weekend House Mirrors River Views

Architect Jefferson Riley was recently asked to renovate a converted ice house that sat less than twenty feet from a bucolic estuary of the Connecticut River. The owners, a Hartford family with two college-aged daughters, felt the small (800 square feet) two-bedroom structure was dark and confining. Only one window was directed toward the river, while all the other windows looked out at a tall hedge and stockade fence that ran along the road, and neighborhood houses.

The owners wanted to renovate the two-story structure into a weekend house that would provide complete privacy, views of the river, plenty of sunshine, sleeping quarters for the family, and a spacious feeling. Enlarging the house, however, was prohibited by the small size of the lot.

Riley's solution was to eliminate all windows on the east side facing the road. The hedge and fence were removed to make space for parking. Then a low wall was extended off the front of the house to create a private yard off the kitchen. To increase the light and airiness of the interior, and to improve its view, the architect added a dormer with a skylight on the west side of the house, facing the river. He then removed about 100 square feet of floor space to create a stairwell court topped by high windows that also face the river. Interior windows on the court, which create a house-within-a-house appearance, impart an open feeling to the living area.

The stair provides access from the living room, kitchen, and dining area on the ground floor to the master bedroom, bathroom, and sleeping loft on the second floor. The kitchen and dining area are separated from the living room by an open stairway. The living room ceiling opens up to the two-story court. As a final touch, Riley placed a many-faceted mirror over the fireplace to reflect multiple images of the river into the living room.

ROAD

RIVER

SITE PLAN   **N**

On a small site *(above)* the two-story house is sandwiched seven feet from the road and nineteen feet from a small river. By removing a hedge and fence, parking space was created on the east side of the house. A low wall with an entry gate extends the roadside façade to the property line and creates space for a private yard directly off the kitchen.

Overleaf: The renovated house contains windows and patio doors on the river, or western side. The dining room opens to a new deck, which contains storage below.

Interior windows allow sunlight to reach all areas and expand the roominess of the renovated house. The interior court, an innovative design, creates the sensation of a village-like setting within the structure.

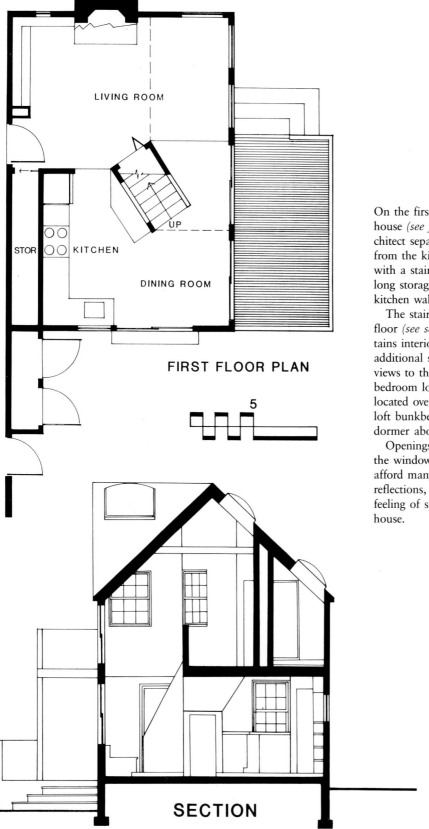

LIVING ROOM

STOR | KITCHEN

UP

DINING ROOM

FIRST FLOOR PLAN

5

SECTION

On the first floor of the vacation house *(see floor plan),* the architect separated the living room from the kitchen and dining area with a stairwell. He also tucked a long storage closet behind the kitchen wall.

The stairwell to the second floor *(see sectional drawing)* contains interior windows that admit additional sunlight and river views to the master bedroom and bedroom loft. Skylights are located over the bathroom and loft bunkbed as well as over the dormer above the court.

Openings in the stairwell and the windows in the interior court afford many river views and reflections, which expand the feeling of spaciousness in the house.

18. This Old Building Serves Many New Functions

In 1980 architect Ralph Gillis inspected several old buildings in New York City with his client, a commercial photographer. Eventually they found a two-story garage and storage building *(below)* which was renovated for about $100 per square foot. The structure now contains an apartment, an office, and a studio that is accessible to, and large enough for, an automobile, a frequent photographic subject.

Although the location and price were right, the building didn't contain quite enough floor space to satisfy all the owner's requirements. Thus, a 700-square-foot mezzanine was inserted into the front portion of the building. This unusual add-on created sufficient space for a multiroom office, a central stairway, and storage. It also separated the busy studio and workrooms on the ground floor from the private living quarters on the second floor.

In order to meet the client's specific need for three distinct functions, the architect's design for the renovation included three entrances. These allow the owner to control access to the studio, office, and apartment.

Throughout the renovated structure are stepped diagonal and angled walls which disguise the true proportions and minimize the box-like appearance of interior spaces. As a result, numerous small and tidy spaces were created for storage and mechanical equipment. Finally, large sliding panels in the living areas allow flexible room arrangements in the open, loft-like apartment.

The brick façade of the original structure *(left)* was retained, but the old garage door and off-center entrance were removed. In their place the architect installed a new garage door, a studio entrance, and, between them, a boldly-framed formal entrance to the residence.

The three entrances to the renovated structure *(left)* include a garage door that opens into a passageway and photographer's studio *(opposite, bottom right)*. The mezzanine add-on, which contains the photographer's office, is visible above the passageway.

A small door on the building's façade allows visitors access to the photographer's office *(opposite, top)*, which contains custom-built storage cabinets and counter space for equipment.

The red-framed entrance in the center of the renovated structure opens into a central stairway *(opposite, bottom left)* which leads to the apartment. The owner also has private access to his photography studio and office by this stairway.

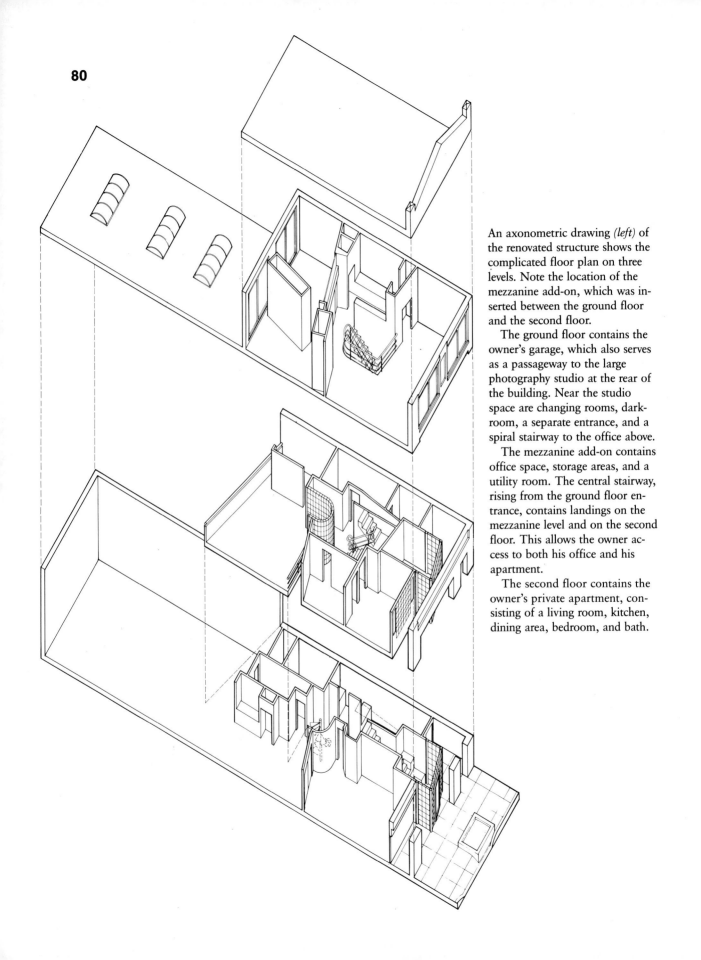

An axonometric drawing *(left)* of the renovated structure shows the complicated floor plan on three levels. Note the location of the mezzanine add-on, which was inserted between the ground floor and the second floor.

The ground floor contains the owner's garage, which also serves as a passageway to the large photography studio at the rear of the building. Near the studio space are changing rooms, darkroom, a separate entrance, and a spiral stairway to the office above.

The mezzanine add-on contains office space, storage areas, and a utility room. The central stairway, rising from the ground floor entrance, contains landings on the mezzanine level and on the second floor. This allows the owner access to both his office and his apartment.

The second floor contains the owner's private apartment, consisting of a living room, kitchen, dining area, bedroom, and bath.

The owner of this unique building knew that living and working at the same address could easily mean one activity spilling into the other. Thus, when renovating and adding to his New York City home and studio, he asked his architect to provide a private entrance *(left)* to his apartment *(top)*. The trim on the glass block entrance and on the central stairway's handrail—painted a playful red—ties together both the materials and the space.

19. Cottage Addition Makes Room for Summer Guests

Architect Leslie Armstrong spent many summers as a child at her grandfather's cottages on Chappaquiddick Island in Martha's Vineyard, Massachusetts. Her grandfather called his summer residence Top Mast Head, but the two structures were known to family members as "the main house" and "the dormitory." The former structure contained a single bedroom, bath, galley kitchen, and family room, while the latter contained two bedrooms and a bath.

In recent years Armstrong's children have enjoyed summer vacations there. So, too, have relatives and their children and friends. And although everyone felt the need for additional space (especially on July 4th holidays) and private corners (especially on rainy days), the

98-year-old paterfamilias resisted a professionally-designed add-on to his summer residence.

Finally, however, he relented, and allowed his granddaughter to design an addition to the dormitory. He stipulated that the new construction had to blend with the shingled Cape Cod-style of the existing buildings. This was achieved by extending the existing roof of the dormitory upward and out in steps *(opposite)*. A new master suite with its own small kitchen and private deck *(below)* was nestled into the bluff on the north side of the structure.

Shortly after the addition to the dormitory was completed, the main house was renovated to accommodate additional guests. The kitchen and bath were combined to form a single kitchen in which several people can work together. Now nearly every room in the expanded complex has outdoor access and private space so that guests don't have to cross one room to reach another. Children can be close to (yet separate from) adults in the same cottage. And meals can be prepared for twelve to fourteen people at a time.

As a final touch, the trim on Top Mast Head was painted a bright orange, which gives the buildings a new sparkle. The color also honors the old man's allegiance to Princeton, from which he graduated in '03!

Working within the Cape Cod style of the existing structure, the architect expanded the roof line of the dormitory in two steps *(opposite)*. The first step covers a utility room and bath, while the second shelters the bedroom/ kitchen addition. Three square windows near the roof's peak admit light and air into the loft bedroom, which was built atop the addition. Nearly every room has both outdoor access and privacy. The architect's 98-year-old grandfather spent his last summer on this persimmon-trimmed deck *(left)*.

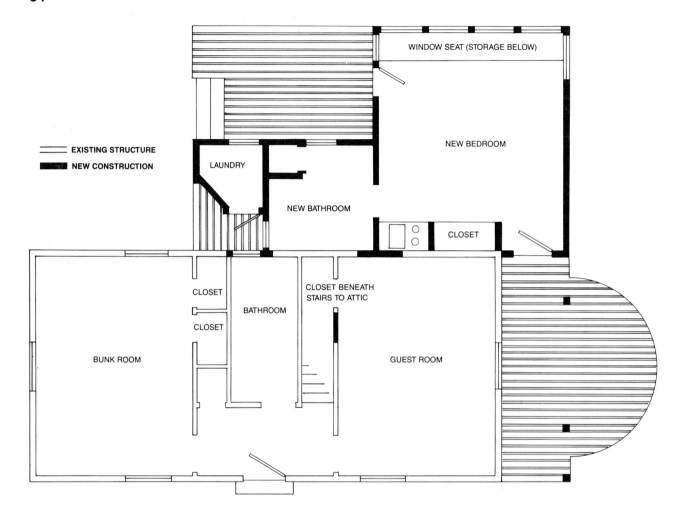

EXISTING STRUCTURE

NEW CONSTRUCTION

WINDOW SEAT (STORAGE BELOW)

NEW BEDROOM

LAUNDRY

NEW BATHROOM

CLOSET

CLOSET

BATHROOM

CLOSET BENEATH STAIRS TO ATTIC

CLOSET

BUNK ROOM

GUEST ROOM

The existing dormitory *(opposite, top)* was a small rectangular structure with two bedrooms and a bath and was situated at the rear of the main house. The floor plan of the dormitory addition *(above)* shows the utility room, bath, and new bedroom with its self-contained kitchen and dining area. Two families can now use this enlarged structure at the same time.

Clamshell molding around the windows and door of the new bedroom *(opposite, below)* is painted a bright green to neatly frame the view of nearby Edgartown Harbor. With only two ferries daily between Chappaquiddick Island and the mainland, construction costs of $70 per square foot reflect high transport expenses.

Armstrong's additon to the dormitory increased the square footage of the summer house by a relatively small amount. However, the new bedroom, with its delightful kitchen and dining area *(top)*, created additional floor space in the loft above the enlarged structure.

The architect used this newfound space for another bedroom *(below)*. Here the clamshell molding is painted a bright yellow. The skylight over the bed and the three square windows (which are located in both gable-end walls) make it an aerie with an inviting presence.

20. Renovation and Addition Form One New Structure

Renovation projects often incorporate additions as important elements in the scheme of upgrading and expanding an old house. Frequently the design of the added portion is so well disguised or fully enveloped by the rest of the house that the combined new structure is experienced as one complete dwelling.

Such was the case in the renovation and addition project shown below and on the following

A diagonal bridge and a two-story "floating core" of kitchen and baths separate the formal living room from the informal family areas of the house.

pages. Designed by architect Kenneth Schroeder for a real-estate developer, the 800-square-foot addition was attached to the rear of a 1,200-square-foot structure. Without changing the width, the finished house is now longer and roomier.

Located near Lincoln Park in Chicago, the original structure was gutted in 1981 and rebuilt at a cost of about $50 per square foot. The new floor plan is organized around a "floating core," which contains a kitchen, closets, and powder room on the first floor and a full bathroom on the second floor. The core separates the formal living areas, oriented to the street, from the informal family areas, oriented to the rear yard. This separation is reinforced by a diagonal bridge across a two-story open space that adjoins a large study over the living room.

In keeping with the design of neighboring houses, Schroeder planned a new brick front and aluminum siding exterior. The new façade also incorporates a large-scale window which, in outline, resembles the two-story buildings in the area.

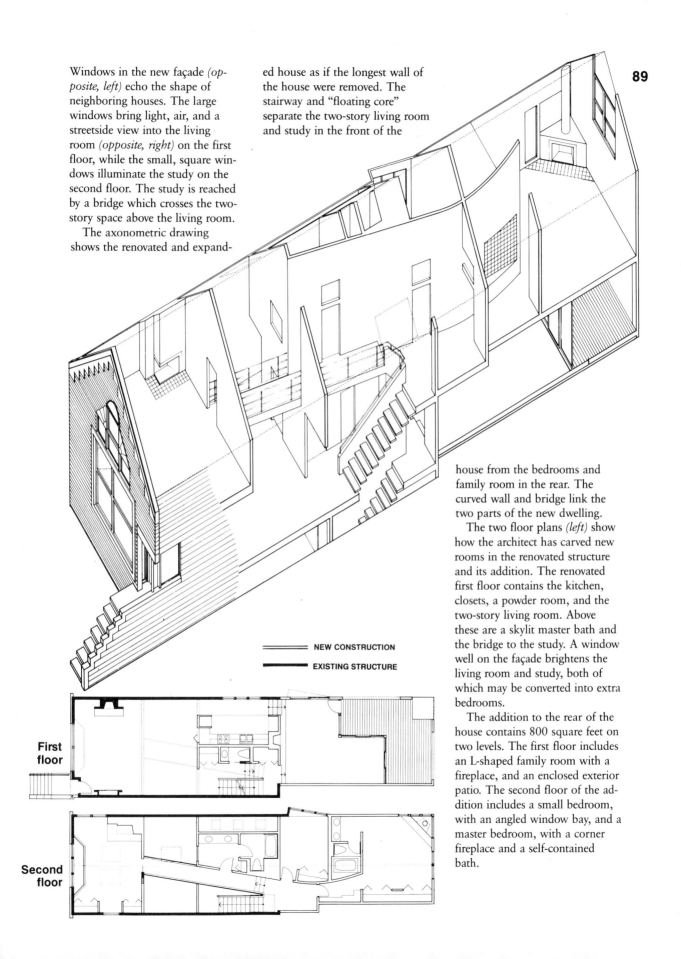

Windows in the new façade *(opposite, left)* echo the shape of neighboring houses. The large windows bring light, air, and a streetside view into the living room *(opposite, right)* on the first floor, while the small, square windows illuminate the study on the second floor. The study is reached by a bridge which crosses the two-story space above the living room.

The axonometric drawing shows the renovated and expanded house as if the longest wall of the house were removed. The stairway and "floating core" separate the two-story living room and study in the front of the house from the bedrooms and family room in the rear. The curved wall and bridge link the two parts of the new dwelling.

The two floor plans *(left)* show how the architect has carved new rooms in the renovated structure and its addition. The renovated first floor contains the kitchen, closets, a powder room, and the two-story living room. Above these are a skylit master bath and the bridge to the study. A window well on the façade brightens the living room and study, both of which may be converted into extra bedrooms.

The addition to the rear of the house contains 800 square feet on two levels. The first floor includes an L-shaped family room with a fireplace, and an enclosed exterior patio. The second floor of the addition includes a small bedroom, with an angled window bay, and a master bedroom, with a corner fireplace and a self-contained bath.

NEW CONSTRUCTION
EXISTING STRUCTURE

First floor

Second floor

21. Dolphin Marks Entry to New Guest Suite

A young family living in an eastern Connecticut house wanted to add a guest suite which would eventually serve as an in-law apartment. The addition, they felt, should be spacious yet clearly separate from the rest of their large, oceanside colonial residence. Rather than build another wing to the house, they asked architect Jefferson Riley of Moore Grove Harper in Essex to plan the apartment in the unused attic space over their garage.

Two obstacles stood in the designer's way, however. First, there was no convenient access from the living areas of the house to the attic. Second, the loft space above the garage was not tall enough to contain a bedroom, sitting room, and full bathroom. To accommodate these requirements Riley installed a stairway along and behind an existing fireplace in the family room. He then raised and extended the roof of the garage to gain needed headroom in the attic. A full bathroom was tucked into a dormer at the north end of the attic space.

The new stairwell created a two-story space where none had existed before. Filled with windows on interior and exterior walls, the sun-filled stairs reach the apartment in two landings. At the top of a third landing, Riley expanded some eave space to create a play loft that overlooks the family room.

In the course of designing the addition, the architect was asked to dress up the existing fireplace in the family room. To celebrate the nearby ocean and its watery residents, Riley fashioned the cherry wood dolphin and fireplace mantel shown on the opposite page.

The guest suite addition, stairway, and play loft added about 750 square feet of living space to the house. The addition cost about $60,000 to build, while the whimsical cherry-wood dolphin and mantel cost about $2,500.

The stairwell *(top)* behind the fireplace is filled with sunlight because the architect added fixed and operable windows on both interior and exterior walls. A large skylight at the top of the space allows sunshine to reach deep into the family room and guest suite, which are located on the north side of the house. The two-story stairwell separates the guest suite from the rest of the house, yet provides convenient access.

The view of the guest suite from the family room *(bottom)* sweeps from the entrance to the stairwell at right, past the interior windows and private entry of the add-on, to the sun-filled windows along the western wall of the play loft.

The architect's use of windows in several sizes and varying configurations on the interior wall creates a village-like atmosphere within the house. The addition is no longer an apartment or guest room. Instead, it becomes a complete dwelling—the tenant's home—within another home. It also makes both spaces appear larger than they actually are.

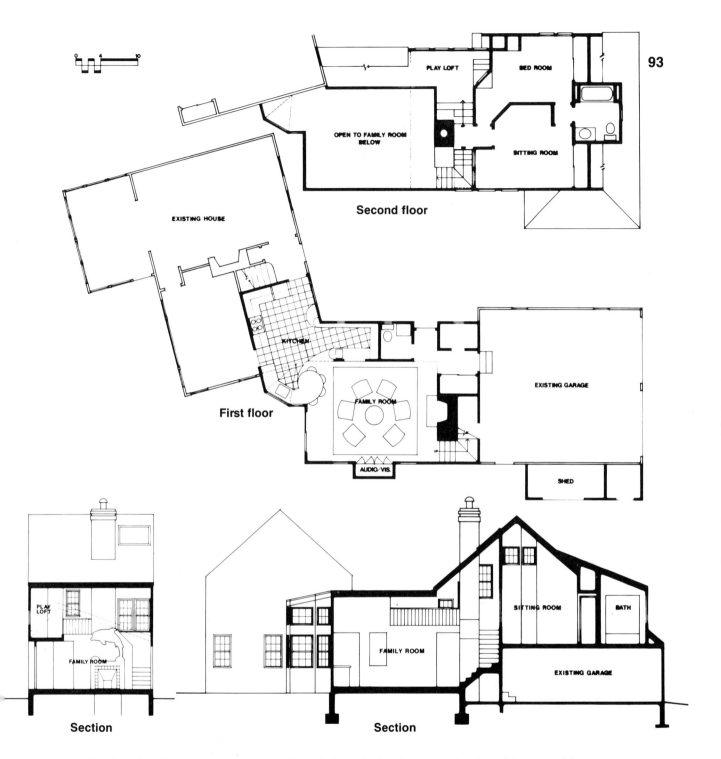

Second floor

EXISTING HOUSE

First floor

KITCHEN

FAMILY ROOM

AUDIO/VIS.

EXISTING GARAGE

SHED

PLAY LOFT

BED ROOM

OPEN TO FAMILY ROOM BELOW

SITTING ROOM

PLAY LOFT

FAMILY ROOM

Section

SITTING ROOM

BATH

FAMILY ROOM

EXISTING GARAGE

Section

As the plan of the first floor shows, the family room is situated between the kitchen and the garage. A stairway surrounds the existing fireplace and reaches the guest suite above the garage and the play loft above the family room *(see plan of second floor)*. The guest suite contains a full bath, a bedroom, and a sitting room.

Sectional drawings reveal the height and location of the guest suite above the garage. A full bath was built ingeniously within a dormer. The arrangement of interior windows along the wall of the addition is also evident.

22. Cherished Home for a New Generation

There are few people who, if they could return to their childhood home, would resist the chance to update its design to meet contemporary notions of efficiency, stylishness, and comfort. When a young family took possession of the husband's earliest home, a turn-of-the-century, foursquare center hall colonial in Fairfax, Virginia, the reality of the place did not match the cherished memories. The 4 x 6-foot laundry room and back entry, circa 1940 eat-in kitchen, and small dining room proved inconvenient and inadequate for the family. With a third child on its way, a major addition to the old house was clearly needed.

When architect David Haresign first met the family, their straightforward requests included a large living space oriented to the pool and rear yard. Upstairs they wanted a large

The rear entrance to the original structure *(left)* brought family and guests into a tiny laundry room and eat-in kitchen. The new entry *(right)* is reached from a car court that extends from the existing driveway. The new entry vestibule provides convenient access to the remodeled kitchen and expanded laundry room.

A new master bedroom *(opposite)* is located on the second floor of the addition. Immediately adjacent to the bedroom are its own bath, dressing room, and two private decks, which allow a discrete view of the garage, pool, and rear yard. Sunlight through the skylight and clerestory windows reaches the family room located under the open balcony at the right.

master bedroom suite with the same privacy and views as the new family room. The addition would allow surveillance of the children by its proximity to the expanded cooking and laundry areas and provide convenient entry at the side of the house.

To fulfill these requests Haresign wrapped the addition around the rear of the house. A new side porch provided automobile access and visually balanced an existing screen porch on the opposite (east) side. Although smaller than the original kitchen, the remodeled room was visually opened to the family room, back yard, and pool. To introduce generous amounts of natural light to the family room, a light well with paired, half-vaulted skylights and clerestory was added.

The floor plans *(below)* show the size and relationship of the addition and the original structure. On the first floor a U-shaped kitchen, which faces the family room dining space, has easy access to the new entry and laundry. The second floor of the addition contains a large master bedroom suite. The new bath and dressing room incorporate quick passage to an adjacent child's room.

From the kitchen the cook's view *(opposite, top)* includes an informal countertop eating area, the new family room, and, through the windows, the pool and rear yard. A double-vaulted light well in the ceiling above the family room admits abundant illumination from skylights in the family room and the master bedroom above.

To mark the edge between the old house and the addition, the architect David Haresign placed the floor of the family room *(opposite, below)* below the existing level. The family room dining area here is convenient to the entry and the kitchen.

First floor

0 1 2 3 4   8   12   16

Second floor

0 1 2 3 4   8   12   16

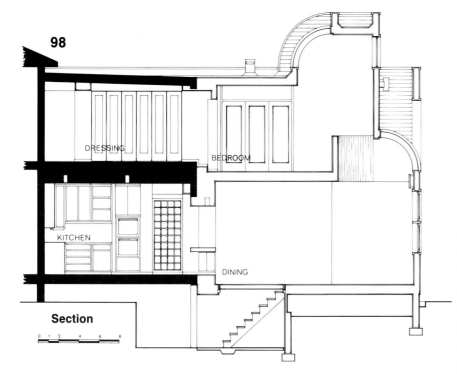

Section

0 1 2 4 6 8

DRESSING

BEDROOM

KITCHEN

DINING

The sectional view *(left)* through the center of the addition and adjacent rooms reveals the structure of the double-vaulted light well. The skylight and the clerestory window in the bedroom introduce natural light which passes through the balcony into the family room below. A barrel-shaped skylight in the ceiling of the family room also contributes natural light to the addition. During summer months this vaulted space operates like a thermal chimney to ventilate the entire addition.

The architect and the owner expressed their modern tastes in the architectural design of the addition, yet complemented the existing structure through the use of clapboards on its exterior *(left)*. This major construction project added approximately 1,200 square feet of living space to the house.

23. Existing Plan Reworked for More Usable Space

For several years architect Thomas Caulfield has been renovating, expanding, and modernizing his own home. Located on a wooded hillside in Berkeley, California, the sixty-year-old structure had a dark and gloomy interior, obsolete kitchen, and 1950s-style remodeled bathroom. The floor plan contained many oddly proportioned spaces, which made circulation difficult. A review of the architect's remedies demonstrates several ways to utilize existing space to the maximum, redesign awkward floor plans, and open a structure to light, view, and air—while preserving the innate charm of an old house.

The biggest trouble spot in the house before remodeling was the kitchen. Originally it was broken into four spaces: broom closet, laundry room, back porch, and a 9 x 11-foot kitchen that was interrupted by stairs to the second floor. By relocating the entry to the stairs and removing walls between rooms, Caulfield created a 10 x 23-foot area with ample work space, an informal dining room, and garden views.

The stairwell was dark and cramped, so the architect removed the second floor ceiling to enlarge the space. In the roof above the stairwell he installed a skylight which illuminates the center of the house. By opening the second floor ceiling, Caulfield obtained access to an unused attic loft space. Reached by a wall-mounted ladder in the second-floor hallway, the loft became a 10 x 15-foot study-guest room. The only structural change in the attic was a window seat "pop-out" which incorporated a peaked end panel of fixed glass and casement windows on each side.

Caulfield also reworked the master bedroom to gain more usable space and an open feeling. A storage area became a 5 x 6-foot dressing corridor with built-in closets. At the end of the corridor, glass doors lead to the porch, which the architect closed in as a sitting room. The interior volume of the bedroom grew when Caulfield knocked out the ceiling to incorporate part of the attic. For structural reasons every other joist was left exposed. To emphasize the new ceiling height, the architect installed a custom-shaped, floor-to-ceiling window.

In consideration of the energy shortage, every wall which was opened up was insulated. Operable skylights provide natural daylight and ventilation, but are double-glazed units to prevent excess heat loss.

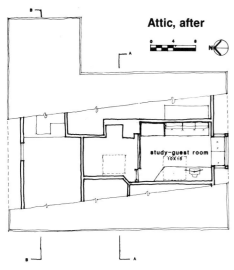

Attic, after

N

The master bedroom *(opposite)* is roomier because the ceiling was extended to the attic rafters. A new window emphasizes the room's height and volume. Alternating rafters were retained to reinforce the walls. A new bathroom replaced a narrow closet on the other side of the room.

Unused attic space was converted to a sun-filled study-guest room *(below)*. Access to this space is via a wall-mounted ladder in the second floor hallway.

The attic floor plan *(left)* shows how a double bed slides into kneewall space to make a couch for daytime seating. On the opposite side of the study there is an access door to storage space behind the kneewall.

The window seat is called a "pop out" because, like a bay window, it juts out when viewed from outside. Overhead a ventilating skylight brightens the room.

study-guest room
10X15

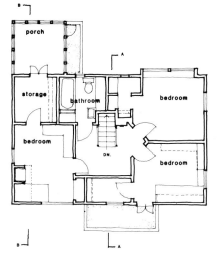

Second floor, before

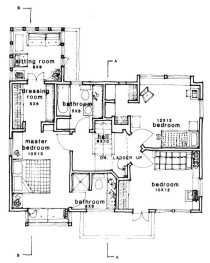

Second floor, after

Without significant additions to the floor space of his home, architect Thomas Caulfield was able to make it spacious, brighter, and more useful. Partitions were relocated, skylights and windows were installed, functional spaces were added, and circulation was improved.

Floor plans *(left)* of the second story before and after the remodeling, which took several years, show the rearrangement of the hall, bathrooms, and master bedroom suite. The skylight above the stair landing in the hall brightens the center of the house. The children's bedrooms and the master bedroom are on opposite sides of the hallway. Space in the narrow closet was refigured as a master bath. The storage area in the master bedroom now serves additionally as a dressing room. The open ceiling over the master bedroom and dressing room brightens and joins both spaces.

The views of the children's bathroom before and after renovation *(left)* show an inventive remodeling of space. The window is simplified and enlarged, the ceiling is raised to the roof rafters, and the skylight brightens the entire space. Tile rises to the ceiling to emphasize the height and volume of a room which did not actually increase in square footage after renovation.

24. Renovation Demonstrates Energy-Saving Methods

Several years ago a group of dedicated community organizers received a small federal grant to purchase a burned-out, abandoned Victorian house in the Eliot neighborhood of Portland, Oregon. Organized as a nonprofit, educational corporation called Responsible Urban Neighborhood Technology, but affectionately known as RUNT, the group renovated the house as a public showcase of energy- and resource-conserving techniques for inner-city residents.

In the process of renovating the Eliot Energy House, as the project is known, workshops were held to offer Portland home owners and tenants an opportunity to learn, through hands-on experience, how to add similar improvements to their own homes. These evening and Saturday workshops were developed around current renovation jobs and important features of the house, including the attic solar greenhouse, passive solar hot-water heating system, waste-water recycling system, low-cost storm windows, weatherization materials, and insulation. Various gardening techniques were taught in the attic solar greenhouse and across the street in a vacant lot that had been turned into a raised-bed community garden.

Hundreds of enthusiastic volunteers, including architect John Perry, who provided the renovation design, have directed or attended these workshops during the three-year construction period. Other local groups, including the Portland Community Design Center, Portland State University, city of Portland, Bureau of Parks, and numerous businesses, contributed home building materials and expertise.

One of the most popular workshops RUNT offered taught participants how to take windows apart, install glass, and caulk and paint. Another workshop dealt with inexpensive but effective home security methods and offered information on installing locks on windows and doors. Garden demonstrations emphasized organic gardening, composting, and French intensive gardening techniques. Garden plots were assigned to interested neighborhood residents for their own use.

With the house renovated and the energy systems in place, the RUNT project began to function as a community library and working model for energy conservation and food production in an urban setting. The organization remains a volunteer-run association of neighbors, so the solar greenhouse has become a teaching tool and a producer of seedlings that are sold to raise money for ongoing programs.

At the left is the abandoned Victorian house as it appeared before it was purchased by RUNT.

Using volunteer labor in hands-on workshops and weekend work days, the hip roof was replaced by a gable-end roof *(opposite)*. The south face of the new roof is glazed and contains an attic solar greenhouse *(below)*. Within this new space are a raised-bed garden of herbs and vegetables, passive solar heat storage in water barrels, and a homemade solar "breadbox" heater which pre-heats domestic hot water.

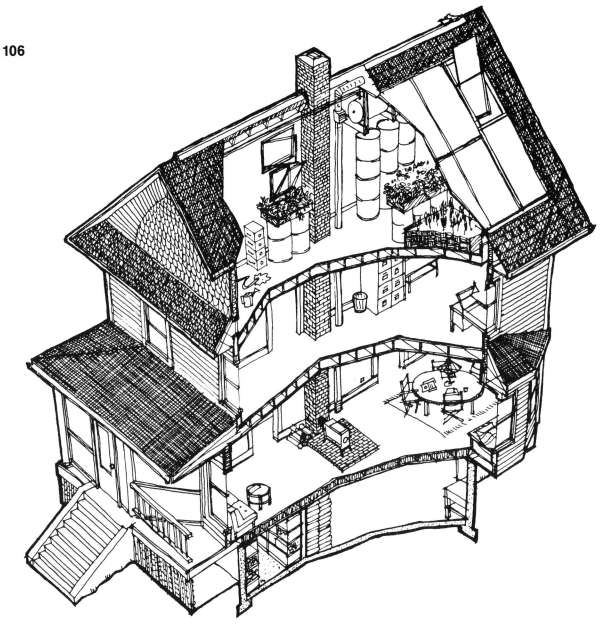

To enter the Eliot Energy House visitors pass through a double-door, or airlock, entry which reduces heat loss in the house. Inside, on the first floor, is a library-resource center, woodstove, bathroom, and kitchen. The compact kitchen contains a "cool closet," which is an insulated, vented cupboard on the north side of the house. It stores bread, cheese, produce, and other foods that do not require refrigeration and allowed installation of a half-sized refrigerator that consumes less electricity than those in typical urban dwellings.

The windows in the house demonstrate several options for saving energy. These include do-it-yourself storm windows, insulated window quilts, and thermal shades.

Shower and kitchen water are reused in the garden. A composting toilet system eliminates water consumption while turning human and kitchen wastes into high-quality fertilizer for the garden.

The second floor contains a large office and library, sleeping room and bathroom. A two-story space over the hall forms a light well which is illuminated by sunshine in the south-facing attic greenhouse.

The solar greenhouse on the third floor provides both heat and food. A low-cost solar water heating system is also located in the attic. The greenhouse, which has been in operation for two years, produces "starter" plants sold to raise funds for RUNT.

The Eliot Energy House was renovated by volunteer labor which was assembled in numerous hands-on workshops by RUNT. In early 1980 the existing hip roof was replaced by a gable-end roof. The roof framing *(top, left)* and glazing panels *(bottom)* for the attic solar greenhouse were installed by work crews who used a buddy system so that experienced carpenters could share their skills and job assignments with inexperienced workers. Tours of the completed house *(top, right)* cover many low-cost energy- conserving and food-producing systems that were incorporated in the design of the renovated structure.

25. A Pig with a Purple Eye Patch

Stucco walls, flat roofs, protruding beams, red-tiled awnings, arched openings, enclosed patios, and pergola-covered terraces are familiar elements of the Spanish style of residential architecture. In Florida and California, where the style is most prevalent, even modest bungalows incorporate these distinguishing traditional characteristics. Yet, when asked to remodel a small cottage built in the Spanish style, the newly-formed San Diego firm Pacific Associates Planners Architects employed these familiar building forms to create a striking new exterior with an imaginative façade.

The client asked architects Richard Dalrymple, James Leighton, and Richard Yen to increase the size of the master bedroom, renovate the kitchen and bathrooms, and develop a studio out of a detached one-car garage located at the rear of the pie-shaped property.

Because of zoning restrictions, all construction work was confined to the existing shell. The total cost of the project was $36,000, which included a new kitchen, all new plumbing and wiring, and two sets of bathroom fixtures.

To the architects' eyes the front of the house resembled a pig. Not an ugly pig, since it appeared quite dignified and matronly, but a pig nonetheless. The bowed canopy reminded them of a pig's snout, the windows its eyes, and the tiled awnings its painted lashes. Delighted with this image of the house, they removed overgrown hedges and a compromising screen door and allowed the façade to stand unfettered in a new coat of paint.

Inspired by their handiwork on the front of the house, the architects used the same building elements to repeat the pig motif on the studio exterior shown on these pages. They then tied the buildings together with a picket fence for yard security. What started as an awkward residence has been transformed into a delightful structure with personality and warmth.

A garage was converted into a studio with its own streetside entrance and façade *(opposite)*. Inspired by a pig motif the architects saw in the design of the façade, they created the visage of a second pig on the studio wall. Under a red-tiled awning this pig wears a purple patch over its right eye. The arched canopy over the entrance forms the pig's snout, while the curved parapet wall ends with the silhouette of a pig's ear.

The rear entrance and pergola *(below, left)* lead to the studio. The trellis *(below, right),* an eyebrow of the pig, provides protection from the sun.

These building elements are twisted, asymmetrical, and colorful. They treat the eye, evoke emotion, and imply gesture in what had been a staid and simple structure.

The front of the house before the remodeling *(above)* needed cleaning and painting. The architects also decided to remove several overgrown shrubs which covered the windows on each side of the entrance.

The revitalized exterior *(below)* uses a bright color on the windows and door and a fresh coat of white paint on the body of the house. While planning the renovation work the architects noted the bowed canopy, which reminded them of a pig's snout. This design motif was repeated in the façade of the converted garage at the rear of the property.

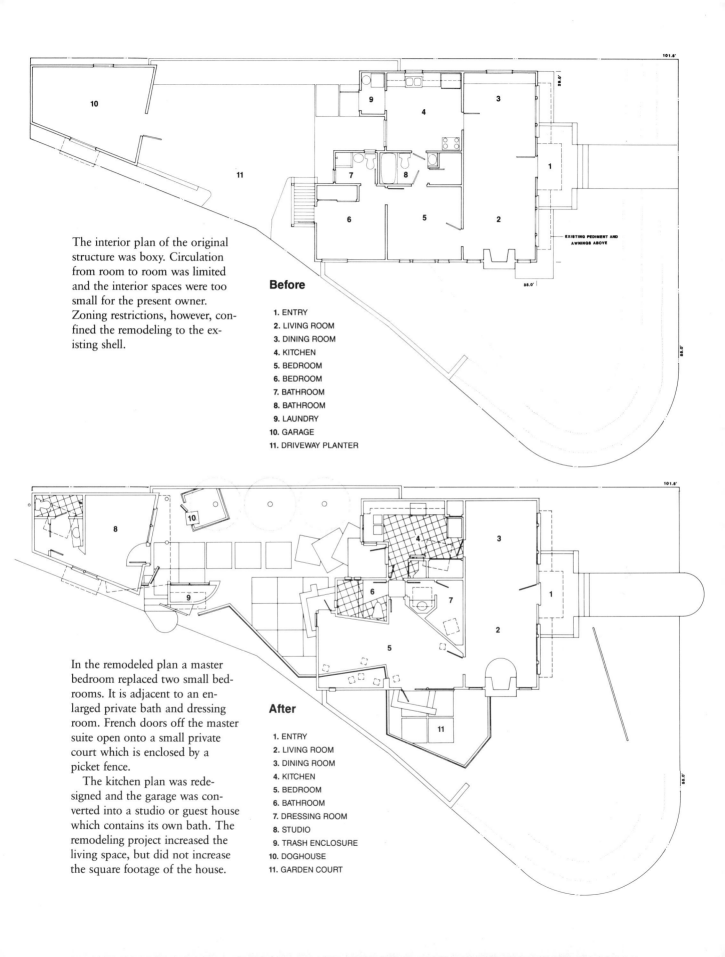

The interior plan of the original structure was boxy. Circulation from room to room was limited and the interior spaces were too small for the present owner. Zoning restrictions, however, confined the remodeling to the existing shell.

Before

1. ENTRY
2. LIVING ROOM
3. DINING ROOM
4. KITCHEN
5. BEDROOM
6. BEDROOM
7. BATHROOM
8. BATHROOM
9. LAUNDRY
10. GARAGE
11. DRIVEWAY PLANTER

In the remodeled plan a master bedroom replaced two small bedrooms. It is adjacent to an enlarged private bath and dressing room. French doors off the master suite open onto a small private court which is enclosed by a picket fence.

The kitchen plan was redesigned and the garage was converted into a studio or guest house which contains its own bath. The remodeling project increased the living space, but did not increase the square footage of the house.

After

1. ENTRY
2. LIVING ROOM
3. DINING ROOM
4. KITCHEN
5. BEDROOM
6. BATHROOM
7. DRESSING ROOM
8. STUDIO
9. TRASH ENCLOSURE
10. DOGHOUSE
11. GARDEN COURT

26. Whimsical "Foliage" Enhances Entryway

This old farmhouse sits prominently atop a hill in central Vermont. Located fifty feet above a country road, it delights passing motorists because of the porch addition that its owner, architect Ted Montgomery, recently designed and built.

Montgomery, who spent $390 for the materials and constructed the add-on by himself, had some practical, aesthetic, and economical reasons for its whimsical design. Foremost was his desire to use the front door, which was hard to reach from the driveway, instead

of the kitchen entry on the side of the house. He also wanted to make a personal statement by modifying the otherwise plain façade. And he provided his own construction labor and used only dimensional lumber because this was an affordable and easy way to work. He felt the low cost and inventive design together would enhance the value of his home.

Because there are only two other man-made structures in view from the house, Montgomery and his wife, Sarah, decided that the porch he would build should celebrate the nearby trees, mountains, and sky. Using 2 x 6 framing lumber, he first built a 4-foot-wide entry deck. Then, using 2 x 4 lumber, he cut, glued, and nailed together four tree trunks. Atop each trunk branches cross and reach upward to a 23-foot-long plate, which was made by splicing and joining 2 x 4 lumber. A pie-shaped plywood disc, which was glued and nailed at the point of the crossing branches, distributes the weight of the roof structure into the tree trunks. Rafters above the tree branches support the foliage (neighbors say they see clouds), which was built from recycled clapboards that were laid atop ¾-inch plywood sheathing. A polyethylene sheet between the plywood and the clapboard helps shed rain water.

Using a circular saw for the dimensional lumber and a reciprocating saw for the clapboard, Montgomery cut all pieces before installation. All joints were caulked before he painted the new porch. This construction work is similar to rough framing in difficulty, although Montgomery paid greater attention to measuring, cutting, and nailing.

Because the porch is shallow and receives only morning sunlight, it was not designed as a sitting area. Instead, it's a good place for plants and is now used as the primary entrance to the house.

Before architect Ted Montgomery designed and built a porch addition to his Vermont home, the front door was seldom used *(left)*. Stone steps from the driveway twelve feet below the front door had long ago been buried in the mud and hillside lawn. Instead, the family used a door to the kitchen wing of the house.

27. Boathouse Expands Lakeside Pleasures

Recently, a suburban New York family purchased a summer house and weekend retreat on a small lake in Westchester County. They were pleased with the main house and guest cottage on the six-acre property. Yet they were dismayed by a dilapidated boathouse and pier that sat at the edge of the lake. Attached to a 20 x 20-foot boat garage, the shower and changing facilities were inadequate for the anticipated crowd of family and guests. What's more, there was little space for sunbathing, swimming, and entertaining.

When they discussed these problems with friends, the owners of the boathouse were referred to Peter and Carol Kurth of Milowitz-Kurth Architects in Scarsdale. Since the boathouse was built before local laws limited waterside construction, the architects realized a sizable addition was possible. Since the family had recently purchased the property, however, funds were tight and the budget for the boathouse add-on was set at $15,000.

The architects added about 300 square feet to the boathouse, which was gutted and remodeled. A new entertainment room, consisting of an efficiency kitchen unit and a dining and seating area, was built. Angled walls are filled with large windows and patio doors that provide a panoramic view of the lake. By law, toilets and heated spaces are not allowed in waterside structures, so the bathing area includes only storage space and a new changing room and shower. The latter area is accessible only from the outdoors so that people in wet bathing suits and sandy feet won't dirty the interior. The boat garage was also restored and a catwalk was rebuilt. The enlarged structure was clad in vertical cedar siding which was painted a light beige.

On two sides of the boathouse the architects added about 1,000 square feet of deck space. Guests have said that sunning on the deck makes them feel as if they're floating on a houseboat even though they're still attached to dry land.

Waterside views of the boathouse include the large new deck *(left)*, the entertainment space with patio door entries, and the boat garage *(below)*. Stone steps down the hillside reach a side entrance to storage facilities. A louvered door opens to the changing room and shower. Without a railing on the deck, the entire structure has a raft-like feeling.

A triangular tie beam *(left)* connects the old structure with the addition. The opening between the beams forms a triangle in which a spiral stair will someday link a roof deck.

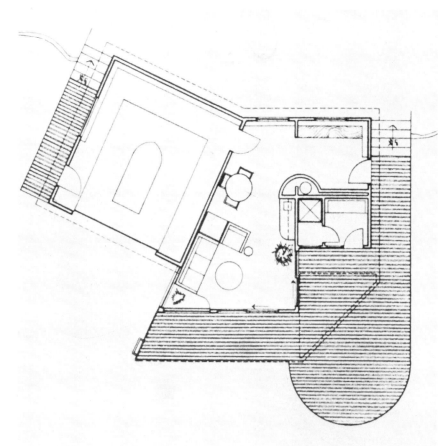

The plan of the enlarged boathouse *(left, top)* shows the arrangement of interior spaces and the relative size of the deck. The changing room and shower are separated from the entertainment area, which incorporates storage space, a kitchen, and dining and seating room. Curved walls and streamlined cabinetry give the entertainment area a nautical feel. A boat garage is reached through a door in the main room and by an outside catwalk. An electric garage door opener provides security in the boat garage. Swimmers can dive from the circular portion of the deck which reaches out over the lake.

Shown just after the addition was completed, the main room *(left)* contains a dramatic view across the lake. By extending the boathouse over the water, the architects captured the floating feeling of a houseboat.

28. Instant Landscaping Makes Lasting Impression

Recently, landscape architect Edward Gaudy was asked to design an attractive garden and patio addition for the owners of a large Tudor-style house in Englewood, New Jersey. When he inspected the grounds, he found a newly-installed pool in the middle of a messy rear yard. What's more, the owners' requirements were monumental and specific: full landscape development of the property; screening from neighborhood yards; and a full-size cabana with bar, storage, showers, and his-and-her bathrooms. They also wanted decking around the pool in decorative pavement, no grass to mow, and a trellised gazebo for an existing patio on the side of the house. Their list included sufficient lighting to provide nighttime atmosphere in the yard while entertaining as-well as an override "panic" switch for instant floodlighting of the property in case of trespassers. In the front yard the owners asked that the existing plain concrete drive be paved over with decorative pavement.

Gaudy was told he could proceed immediately with his design for the property so long as he could complete the construction job by July 4th. The owners planned an important party for that date, and they wanted to hold it around the pool. Gaudy was given full charge of the project, a retainer for his design and supervisory work, and payments every fifteen days for the construction work.

What followed that spring was a fevered rush: building permits were obtained; sewer connections were made through 18-inch concrete foundations; electrical and plumbing tie-ins were established; foundations for walls and steps were dug and laid; a concrete base was poured for all brick work around the pool; and the cabana was installed.

Meanwhile, Gaudy visited local nurseries to select the many shrubs and trees for the property, an enormous task in itself. To his great credit the architect finished the $250,000 landscape project on July 3rd, a day before the deadline.

Above: How the site looked at the outset of the project.

Gaudy's plan *(below)* called for a brick driveway and cobblestone court which leads a visitor to a side gate that matches the Tudor architecture of the house. There, a brick walk among rhododendrons, azaleas, and small evergreens meanders to a set of curved steps that allow a full view of the pool and cabana.

The rear yard contains several levels of bricked terraces and various functional zones. These include a trellised gazebo, an outdoor dining area, a twin cabana, a decorative brick wall to hide mechanical equipment, and abundant seating and sunning areas around the pool and whirlpool spa.

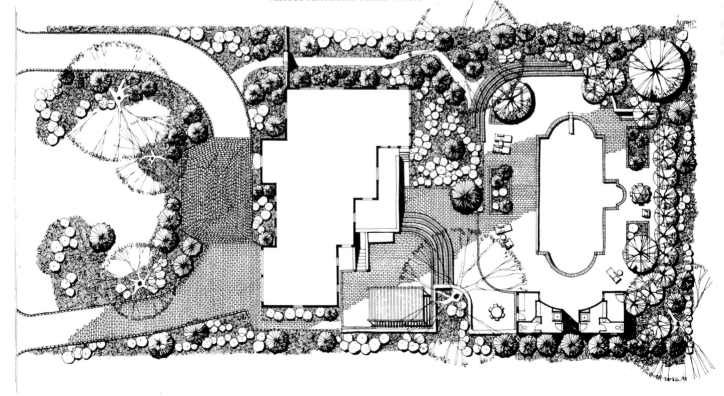

In less than four months, landscape architect Edward Gaudy transformed the rear yard and pool of this Tudor-style house *(below and opposite, bottom).*

In addition to a paved brick patio deck and twin cabana, the architect added the shrubs and trees to the yard. These include azaleas, rhododendrons and mountain laurel for flowering accents, and junipers, Japanese yews, Austrian pines and Japanese pines for their year-round greenery. A large Japanese red maple is a natural focal point of the patio and landscape addition.

The floor plan of the cabana *(opposite, top)* shows how Gaudy provided multiple functions in a pair of 15 x 13-foot wood frame structures. He included storage space, a cocktail bar with cooktop, changing rooms, showers, and his-and-her bathrooms. Cabana units face the yard for privacy.

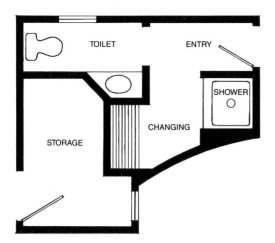

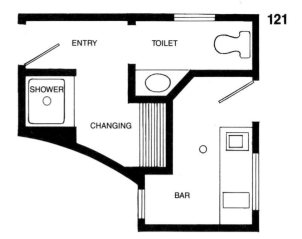

29. Hexagonal Design Satisfies Revised Expectations

Add-ons don't just happen. They evolve from original ideas, the needs and desires of home owners, and from discussions between architects and their clients. But once the design is settled, the construction job takes on a life of its own that even veterans of the process say can't be predicted.

When a Cincinnati couple wanted to add a garden room to the rear of their suburban home, they brought their idea for a circular addition to architect Stan Better. The add-on should offer panoramic views of the backyard, they told him, and complement the existing house in design and color. They also wanted to heat and cool the room with controls that were independent from the existing central system. According to their wishes, Better began designing a circular addition, but the plan was rejected because of its complexity and high cost.

In reassessing their design ideas with the architect, the couple settled on a hexagonal add-on. Large window walls would offer the back-yard views they wanted and the addition could be finished to match the rest of the house. It even met their construction budget of $20,000. The hexagonal structure, however, proved almost as complex as the circular addition. The six-sided shape appears simple to construct, but requires many time-consuming cuts in framing lumber and finishing materials. Fortunately, Better's remodeling crews were familiar with complicated framing cuts. The architect also specified several economic building materials for the job.

The 300-square-foot garden room was built atop an existing concrete patio deck. Aluminum windows in stock sizes were utilized for their economical cost. Aluminum siding was chosen for the exterior of the addition because it matched the existing house and can be bent to the configurations desired. Insulated walls were finished with drywall and white paint which made the room appear big and bright. Small skylights were installed in the ceiling to further illuminate and expand the space.

The construction project was completed in the summer of 1980. Although the wife originally planned to use the addition as *her* garden room, the husband liked the space so much he took it over as *his* study. Because a through-the-wall heating/air conditioning unit was installed, the owners can enjoy *their* room year-round.

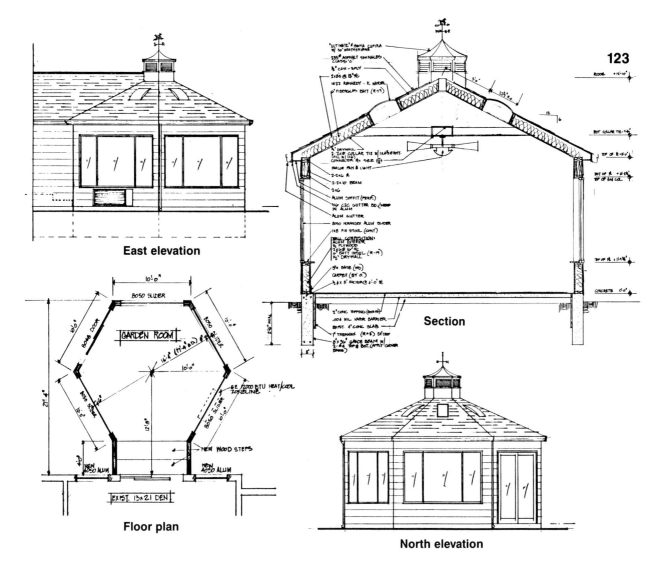

East elevation

Floor plan

Section

North elevation

The finished design of the garden room is shown in the sectional drawing and in the east and north elevations. The general layout of the room is illustrated in the floor plan. Because the garden room was built with an independent heating/air conditioning system, the walls of the add-on contain six inches of fiberglass insulation and double-glazed window units. A ceiling fan is employed to circulate the air in the room.

Left: The existing patio, site of the addition, has been broken up and a new foundation is being laid.

The construction of the hexagonal garden room is seen in the photographs at the left. First, 2 x 6 plates were attached to the existing house wall and across the concrete patio. Main bearing posts and wall studs were then built and box-beam headers were installed across the window and door openings.

Next, ½-inch plywood sheets were nailed on walls. The roof collar and ridge were tied into the add-on structure.

An interior view shows the hub and rafter system that the construction crew cut and fit into place at the job site. Creating this rafter system was a labor-intensive process.

Finally, window and door openings are ready for the installation of aluminum units. A cupola was installed atop the roof hub to provide ventilation for the structure.

The completed garden room looks deceivingly simple, since the frame is covered by siding and the rafters are covered by roofing. The expense of a complicated framing job was offset by the selection of economical building materials such as aluminum siding, asphalt shingles, aluminum windows, and interior drywall with a paint finish.

Small skylights were installed in the ceiling to make the room appear big and bright, and double-glazing will cut down on heat loss in winter.

125

30. Music Inspires Dramatic Pavillion

Additions, like the houses they join, reflect characteristics of the people who design and build them. When the owner of the house on these pages consulted with architects Peter and Carol Kurth, there was little doubt that the addition would strike a musical theme. In fact, since the owner makes his living producing and recording music, a piano was sculpturally embodied in the design of the add-on, which is located in Westchester County, New York.

The architects were asked to design a large room that would house the owner's grand piano, sophisticated recording equipment, and unusual art collection. The owner even helped with the acoustic design and engineering of the interior space. He knew, for example, that he didn't want any box-like spaces or perpendicular walls. Instead, he asked for an oak ceiling with structural oak beams which fan out above the piano and create an acoustic shell. Under this shell the piano was set on a stage, with a seating platform nearby.

A restrictive setback line and the architects' sensitivity to the existing house contributed to the exterior shape of the addition *(below)*. One side was designed to resemble the appearance of an open piano, while the other façade simulated the instrument's curved forms. Dark-stained vertical siding, cedar shingle roofing, and fieldstone walls link the addition's exterior finish to the existing structure.

The curved wall was punctuated by a band of glass block, which sends diffuse light into the room and forms a glow around the piano. Triangular clerestories allow high, indirect light to reach deep within the space and dramatize the sloping planes of the oak ceiling with varying levels of light and mood.

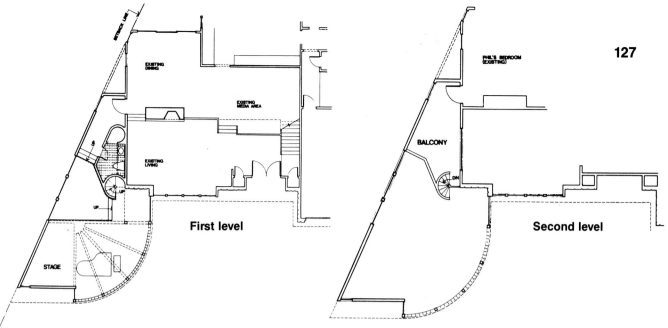

First level

Second level

The piano pavillion addition resembles a piano in plan *(above)* and elevation. The piano is set on a stage-like platform *(overleaf)* under an oak-beamed ceiling. A spiral stair leads up to the balcony *(bottom, left)* with a spectacular view of the piano area as well as glimpses of the surrounding wooded site. Acoustically and physically, the addition is separated from the existing house, so both areas retain their privacy.

Clerestory windows *(left, center)* along the setback wall represent the open piano and introduce changing light to the interior space. At night, lights on the inside make the addition glow.

Part of the owner's extensive art collection is seen at the left. The completed project added nearly 1,000 square feet of floor space to the existing house and cost about $90 per square foot to build in 1981.

SPECIFICATIONS AND
SOURCE DIRECTORY

National and regional suppliers of products and services used in the add-ons described in this book are listed below only by name; their full addresses and telephone numbers can be found in the Add-On Source Directory (pages 145-158).

1. Curved Sun Room Brightens Adobe Home

Designer and Subcontractor: Valerie Walsh, Solar Horizon, P.O. Box 8913, Santa Fe, NM 87504
Type of Add-On: Sun room
Area Added: 200 square feet
Approximate Cost: $7,000
Year Completed: 1978
Building Materials and Furnishings:
 Lighting fixtures—Artesanos, Santa Fe, NM
 Roof Glazing—General Electric Company
 Windows—Andersen Corporation

2. Oriel Brings Light and View to Victorian Dining Room

Designer and Subcontractor: James and Beth Facinelli, Restorations Unlimited, Inc., 24 West Main St., Elizabethville, PA 17023
Type of Add-On: Oriel window
Area Added: 200 square feet
Year Completed: 1979
Building Materials and Furnishings:
 Cabinets—Rich Craft Custom Kitchens, Robesonia, PA
 Millwork, siding, and carpentry—designer/subcontractor
 Windows—Pella/Rolscreen Company

3. Farmhouse Renovation Adds Studio and Greenhouse

Designer: Joe Hylton, Joe Hylton & Associates—Architects, 313 E. Boyd St., Norman, OK 73069

Subcontractor: Owner and Mitch Baroff, Sun Energy Company, Norman, OK

Type of Add-On: Studio and greenhouse

Area Added: 600 square feet

Year Completed: 1983

Building Materials and Furnishings:
Air conditioning unit—Carrier Air Conditioning
Bath cabinetry and shower—Sunnay Shape, Norman, OK
Bath fixtures, lighting fixtures, and cedar shingles—Renovator's Supply
Doors—Holiday Finishing Company, Norman, OK
Flooring—Quality Floors, Norman, OK
Greenhouse—Lord & Burnham; Moesel's Horticultural Haven, Oklahoma City, OK
Insulation—Owens-Corning
Kitchen cabinets—Don Krestinger, Norman, OK
Kitchen countertops—Formica
Molding and trim—Slocomb's Millwork, Norman, OK
Oven and range—Jenn-Air
Roofing—Carry Lumber, Norman, OK
Sauna and hot tub—California Cooperage
Solar heating equipment—Grumman Energy Systems
Windows—Bill Law Window Company, Norman, OK
Wood stove—The Energy Store, Norman, OK

4. Seaside Space for Home Hobbyists

Designer: Alfredo De Vido, Alfredo De Vido Associates, 699 Madison Ave., New York, NY 10021

Type of Add-On: Greenhouse, shop, and gallery

Area Added: 2,700 square feet

Approximate Cost: $270,000

Year Completed: 1983

Building Materials and Furnishings:
Air conditioning units—Carrier Air Conditioning
Bath fixtures—American-Standard
Greenhouse—custom built
Hardware—Schlage Lock Company
Roof windows—Velux-America

Stair systems—custom built
Vanity cabinets—custom built
Windows—Andersen Corporation

5. Guest House Matches Adobe-Style Home

Designer: Robert W. Peters, AIA, 10 Tumbleweed NW, Albuquerque, NM 87120
Type of Add-On: Guest house
Area Added: 967 square feet
Approximate Cost: $71,000
Year Completed: 1980
Building Materials and Furnishings:
   Bath faucets and shower—Speakman Company
   Bath fixtures—American-Standard
   Greenhouse—custom built
   Kitchen appliances—Dwyer Products Corporation
   Kitchen countertops—Formica
   Solar heat/water storage—custom built
   Tile—Agency Tile
   Windows—Marvin Windows

6. A New Angle on Suburban Living

Designer: Stan Better, AIA, Stan Better Construction Co., Inc., 8473 Fernwell Dr.,
   Cincinnati, OH 45231
Subcontractors: Zimmer Heating and Air Conditioning, Cincinnati, OH; Advanced
   Electric Service, Cincinnati, OH
Type of Add-On: Family room
Area Added: 250 square feet
Approximate Cost: $32,000
Year Completed: 1983
Building Materials and Furnishings:
   Countertops—Formica
   Drywall—U.S. Gypsum Company
   Flooring—Armstrong World Industries
   Gutters and downspouts—Alcoa
   Insulation—Owens-Corning
   Lumber and building supplies—Queen City Lumber Company, Cincinnati, OH
   Paneling—Weyerhaeuser
   Roof shingles—Celotex Corporation
   Skylights—Skymaster

7. Greenhouse Brightens City House Interiors

Designer: Frank Caminiti, Bert Stern, and Nick Michaels, Architrave, 65 Bleecker St., New
  York, NY 10012
Type of Add-On: Greenhouse
Area Added: 272 square feet
Approximate Cost: part of a $250,000 renovation
Year Completed: 1983
Building Materials and Furnishings:
  Air conditioning unit—Carrier Air Conditioning
  Cabinetry—custom built by George Dorn-Weichun, New York, NY
  Greenhouse—Lancer Metals, Long Island City, NY
  Molding and trim—custom made by Christopher Whitney, New York, NY
  Siding and repairs—J. Gatti & Sons, New York, NY
  Flooring—Country Floors

8. A Sunny Addition for Family Entertaining

Designer: Grayson Ferrante, Princeton Energy Group, 375 Ewing St., Princeton, NJ 08540
Type of Add-On: Greenhouse/family room
Area Added: 200 square feet
Year Completed: 1982
Building Materials and Furnishings:
  Plastic roof glazing—CY/RO Industries

9. Oak-Trimmed Addition Replaces Austere Kitchen

Designer: Glen William Jarvis, AIA, 3104 Shattuck Ave., Berkeley, CA 94705
Contractor: Andy Anderson, Oakland, CA
Type of Add-On: Kitchen/family room
Area Added: 174 square feet
Year Completed: 1980
Building Materials and Furnishings:
  Cabinetry—oak storage cabinet custom built by contractor
  Dishwaser—KitchenAid
  Faucet—Chicago Faucet Company
  Flooring—custom oak flooring built by contractor
  French doors—custom built by contractor
  Garbage disposal—In-Sink-Erator
  Refrigerator—Frigidaire
  Sink—American-Standard
  Windows—Andersen Corporation

10. Facilities Expanded for Efficient Entertaining

Designer: Donald Silvers, CKD, 137 North Detroit, Los Angeles, CA 90036
Type of Add-On: Kitchen plan re-worked and modernized
Year Completed: 1981
Building Materials and Furnishings:
　Cabinets—Wood Mode Cabinetry
　Convection oven and barbeque grill—Jenn-Air
　Cooktop and oven—Chambers Corporation
　Dishwasher—Maytag
　Gargage disposal—In-Sink-Erator
　Mixing center—Nutone
　Refrigerator-freezer—White-Westinghouse
　Sinks and fittings—Kohler
　Trash compactor—Thermador/Waste King
　Ventilating hood and roof fan—custom made

11. Kitchen Expansion Updates Town House

Designer: James Oleg Kruhly, AIA, 1621 Cypress St., Philadelphia, PA 19103
Type of Add-On: Breakfast room
Area Added: 105 square feet
Approximate cost: $32,000
Year Completed: 1979
Building Materials and Furnishings:
　Air conditioning—General Electric
　Cabinets—custom designed
　Cooktop—General Electric
　Countertops—Formica
　Dishwasher—KitchenAid
　Lighting fixtures—Lightolier
　Oven—Thermador/Waste King
　Refrigerator—Sub-Zero Freezer Company

12. "Bump Out" Forms Cook's New Space

Designers: Kenneth J. Abler and Jacob Sofer, Architectural Design Group, 720 University
　Ave., Palo Alto, CA 94301
Contractor: TLG Construction Company, Los Gatos, CA
Type of Add-On: Kitchen addition and remodeling
Area Added: 48 square feet

Approximate Cost: $30,000
Year Completed: 1982
Building Materials and Furnishings:
    Cabinets and butcher block insert—custom built
    Cooktop—Modern Maid
    Countertops—Formica
    Dishwasher—General Electric Company
    Flooring—custom-installed 5/16-inch strip oak
    Hardware—Schlage Lock Company
    Lighting fixtures—General Electric Company (custom order)
    Microwave oven—Sharp Electronics Corporation
    Oven—Frigidaire
    Windows—Pozzi Window Company

13. Making Room for More Than One Cook

Designer: James W. Krengel, CKD, Kitchens By Krengel, Inc., 1688 Grand Ave., St. Paul, MN 55105
Type of Add-On: Kitchen
Area Added: 190 square feet
Year Completed: 1981
Building Materials and Furnishings:
    Cooktop, microwave oven, and ventilation unit—Thermador/Waste King
    Countertop—Formica
    Dishwasher, disposal, and trash compactor—KitchenAid
    Icemaker—Scotsman Ice Systems
    Refrigerator and freezer—Sub-Zero Freezer Company
    Sink and fittings—Kohler Company

14. Gazebo Inspires New Breakfast Room

Designer: Glen William Jarvis, AIA, 3104 Shattuck Ave., Berkeley, CA 94705
Contractor: Charles Kuhn, Inc., Novato, CA
Type of Add-On: Breakfast room
Area Added: 120 square feet
Approximate Cost: $20,000
Year Completed: 1982
Building Materials and Furnishings:
    Cabinets, doors, windows, and flooring—custom made by contractor

15. Relocated Entry Invites New Look at Old House

Designer: Stephen Lasar, AIA, Stephen Lasar Architects, P. O. Box 1401, New Milford, CT 06776
General Contractor: Neufeld-Lasar Design Build Company, New Milford, CT
Subcontractors: Framing—Picton Construction Company, Washington Depot, CT; Trim and Cabinetry—Allen Lord Custom Woodworks, New Milford, CT
Type of Add-On: Bedroom expansion and renovation
Area Added: 255 square feet
Approximate Cost: $50,000
Year Completed: 1983
Building Materials and Furnishings:
    Bath fixtures—Kohler
    Cabinetry—custom built
    Doors—exterior, Peachtree Doors; interior, C-E Morgan
    Flooring—Florida Tile
    Hardware—Schlage Lock Company
    Lighting fixtures—Lightolier
    Roof windows—Velux-America and custom built
    Windows—Marvin Windows (custom built)

16. Summer Bungalow Raised to New Heights

Designer: James Oleg Kruhly, AIA, 1621 Cypress St., Philadelphia, PA 19103
Type of Add-On: Two-story addition with garage
Area Added: 625 square feet
Approximate Cost: $90,000
Year Completed: 1979
Building Materials and Furnishings:
    Air conditioning unit—Friedrich Air Conditioning & Refrigeration Company
    Bath fixtures and hardware—Kohler
    Cabinetry—custom made
    Countertops—Formica Corporation
    Hardware—Kwikset
    Kitchen sink—Moen
    Refrigerator—Sub-Zero Freezer Company
    Windows—Andersen Corporation

17. Weekend House Mirrors River Views

Designer: Jefferson Riley, AIA, Moore Grover Harper, Essex, CT 06426
Type of Add-On: Interior renovation
Approximate Cost: $40,000
Year Completed: 1978
Building Materials and Furnishings:
   Windows—Andersen Corporation

18. This Old Building Serves Many New Functions

Designer: Ralph Gillis, AIA, Gillis Associates, 156 Fifth Ave., New York, NY 10010
Contractor: L. H. Davis, New York, NY
Type of Add-On: Studio and office
Area Added: 700 square feet
Approximate Cost: $70,000
Year Completed: 1982
Building Materials and Furnishings:
   Air conditioner—Carrier Corporation
   Bath fixtures and hardware—Kohler Company; American-Standard; Jacuzzi Whirlpool
      Bath
   Cabinetry—custom built
   Hardware—Ironmonger, Chicago, IL; Schlage Lock Company; Stanley Hardware
   Lighting fixtures—Kurt Verson, Westwood, NJ; Lightolier; LSI, Inc., New York, NY;
   Wiremold, New York, NY; Infranor, Berlin, CT.
   Railings—custom fabricated steel
   Stairs—Duvinage, New York, NY
   Walls—Pittsburgh-Corning Corporation (glass block)
   Windows—Duratherm Window Corporation

19. Cottage Addition Makes Room for Summer Guests

Designer: Leslie Armstrong, AIA, Butler Rogers Baskett, 381 Park Ave. S., New York,
   NY 10016
Interior Designers: Thomas A. Koloski and Robin Gitomer
General Contractor: Edward Warsyk, Edgartown, MA
Type of Add-On: Guest house
Area Added: 400 square feet
Approximate Cost: $28,000
Year Completed: 1980

Building Materials and Furnishings:
    Bath fixtures—American-Standard
    Cabinetry—custom built by Roy Hayes, Edgartown, MA
    Countertops—Formica Corporation
    Flooring—Edward Warsyk, Edgartown, MA
    Kitchen sink—Kohler Company
    Laundry Equipment—White-Westinghouse
    Oven—General Electric Company
    Windows—custom built

20. Renovation and Addition Form One New Structure

Designer: Kenneth Schroeder, Kenneth Schroeder & Associates, 714 South Dearborn, Chicago, IL 60605
Developer: Wronkiewicz and Ross, Chicago, IL
Contractor: John Wronkiewicz, Chicago, IL
Type of Add-On: Two-story addition
Area Added: 800 square feet
Approximate Cost: $40,000
Year Completed: 1981
Building Materials and Furnishings:
    Air conditioning units—Bryant Air Conditioning
    Bath fixtures and hardware—Bathwares, Chicago, IL; Kohler Company
    Cabinetry—Macor
    Countertops—Formica
    Dishwasher—KitchenAid
    Doors—C-E Morgan (interior)
    Fireplace—Majestic
    Roof windows—Velux America
    Windows—Biltbest Windows

21. Dolphin Marks Entry to New Guest Suite

Designer: Jefferson Riley, AIA, Moore Grover Harper, Essex, CT 06426
Type of Add-On: Guest suite
Area Added: 750 square feet
Approximate Cost: $60,000
Year Completed: 1982
Building Materials and Furnishings:
    Windows—Andersen Corporation

22. Cherished Home for a New Generation

Designer: David Haresign, Dewberry & Davis, 8401 Arlington Blvd., Fairfax, VA 22031
General Contractor: Henry D. Webb
Structural Engineer: John Welch, P.E.
Mechanical Engineer: Art Carlson
Type of Add-On: Family room and bedroom
Area Added: 1200 square feet
Approximate Cost: $82,000
Year Completed: 1982
Building Materials and Furnishings:
Cabinets—custom built
Cooktop range—Jenn-Air Corporation
Countertops—Formica Corporation
Dishwasher—KitchenAid
Flooring—Henry D. Webb
Garbage disposal—In-Sink-Erator
Hardware—Schlage Lock Company
Insulation—Owens-Corning Fiberglas Corporation
Lighting fixtures—Lightolier
Oven—Hotpoint
Refrigerator—Whirlpool
Siding—Masonite Corporation
Skylights—Rohm & Haas Company; installed by Herndon Lumber & Millwork,
    Herndon, PA
Walls—Pittsburgh-Corning Corporation (glass block)
Windows—Caradco

23. Existing Plan Reworked for More Usable Space

Designers: Thomas and Anne Caulfield, Peters Clayberg & Caulfield, 370 Brannan St.,
    San Francisco, CA 94107
Type of Add-On: Loft addition
Area Added: 150 square feet
Year Completed: 1982
Building Materials and Furnishings:
Bath fixtures and hardware—Delta Faucet Company
Cabinets—designed and built by owners
Countertops—Formica Corporation (oak edging by owner)
Dishwasher—KitchenAid

Garbage disposal—Thermador/Waste King
Hardware—Schlage Lock Company
Insulation—Owens-Corning Fiberglas Corporation
Laundry equipment and range—Whirlpool
Oven and refrigerator—General Electric Company
Skylights—O'Keefe's, Inc.

24. Renovation Demonstrates Energy-Saving Methods

Designer: John Perry, AIA, 2917 NE Alameda, Portland, OR 97212
Plumbing Contractor: Ca-Sun, Portland, OR
Kitchen Contractor: Neil Kelly Designers/Remodelers, Inc., Portland, OR
Type of Add-On: Greenhouse and renovation
Total Area Involved: 1,926 square feet
Year Completed: 1983
Building Materials and Furnishings:
  Cabinetry—Neil Kelly Designers/Remodelers (custom built)
  Flooring—Armstrong World Industries
  Greenhouse—custom built
  Gutters and downspouts—Plastmo
  Hardware—Kwikset
  Heating system—Lennox Industries
  Insulation—CertainTeed Corporation; Owens-Corning Fiberglas Corporation
  Lighting fixtures—Lightolier
  Molding and trim—Mike Heeley, Portland, OR
  Range—Whirlpool
  Skylights—Velux America
  Solar heating equipment—Honeywell, Incorporated

25. A Pig with a Purple Eye Patch

Designer: Richard Dalrymple, James Leighton, and Richard Yen, Pacific Associates
  Planners Architects, Inc., 614 Fifth Ave., Suite B, San Diego, CA 92101
Contractors: John McKeivek and John Sheffield, San Diego, CA
Type of Add-On: House renovation and garage conversion
Approximate Cost: $36,000
Year Completed: 1982

26. Whimsical "Foliage" Enhances Entryway

Designers: Ted and Sarah Montgomery, Local Star Ltd., Cox Brook Rd., Northfield, VT 05663
Type of Add-On: Porch
Area Added: 48 square feet
Approximate Cost: $390
Year Completed: 1983
Building Materials and Furnishings:
  locally-available lumber and clapboards; owner-built

27. Boathouse Expands Lakeside Pleasures

Designers: Peter C. Kurth, AIA, and Carol J. W. Kurth, AIA, Milowitz-Kurth Architects, 455 Central Ave., Scarsdale, NY 10583
Contractor: MKC Development Corporation, Scarsdale, NY
Type of Add-On: Boat house expansion
Area Added: 300 square feet
Approximate Cost: $15,000
Year Completed: 1981
Building Materials and Furnishings:
  Doors and windows—Acorn Building Components
  Gutters and Downspouts—custom built
  Hardware—Schlage Lock Company
  Insulation—Owens-Corning Fiberglas Corporation
  Kitchen appliance unit—Dwyer Products Corporation
  Siding—Rings End Lumber, Lewisboro, NY

28. Instant Landscaping Makes Lasting Impression

Designers: Edward Gaudy and James Hadley, Gaudy-Hadley Associates, 137 Piermont Ave., South Nyack-on-Hudson, NY 10960
Contractors: Robert M. Baver & Associates, Carmel, NY: Taylor Construction, North Salem, NY
Type of Add-On: Twin cabana (and extensive landscaping)
Total Area Involved: 16,500 square feet
Approximate Cost: $250,000
Year Completed: 1981

29. Hexagonal Design Satisfies Revised Expectations

Designer: Stan Better, AIA, Stan Better Construction Company, Inc., 8473 Fernwell Dr., Cincinnati, OH 45231
Contractors: Advanced Electric Service, Cincinnati, OH; Zimmer Heating and Air Conditioning, Cincinnati, OH
Type of Add-On: Garden room
Area Added: 300 square feet
Approximate Cost: $20,000
Year Completed: 1980
Building Materials and Furnishings:
   Air conditioning and heating systems—General Electric Company
   Insulation—Owens-Corning Fiberglas Corporation
   Lumber and building supplies—Queen City Lumber Company, Cincinnati, OH
   Roofing—Celotex Corporation
   Skylights—Skymaster
   Windows and doors—Norandex Aluminum Building Products, Cleveland, OH

30. Music Inspires Dramatic Pavillion

Designer: Peter C. Kurth, AIA and Carol J. W. Kurth, AIA, Milowitz-Kurth Architects, 455 Central Ave., Scarsdale, NY 10583
Contractor: MKC Development Corporation, Scarsdale, NY
Type of Add-On: Music room
Area Added: 1,000 square feet
Approximate Cost: $90,000
Year Completed: 1981
Building Materials and Furnishings:
   Bath fixtures—Kohler
   Bathroom tiles—Bedford Tile Company, Bedford, NY
   Doors, stairway, molding, and trim—Rings End Lumber, Lewisboro, NY
   Flooring—Geysir Flooring Company, Bedford, NY
   Lighting fixtures—Lightolier
   Walls—PPG Industries (glass block)
   Windows—Andersen Corporation

ADD-ON SOURCE DIRECTORY

The following list of manufacturers and suppliers has been divided into subject categories for easy reference. All of the companies listed are national or regional organizations; most will be happy to supply information about their products and about local suppliers of those products. Local suppliers whose products and services were used in the construction of the add-ons described in this book are listed in the Project Specifications section (pages 131-143).

Bathroom Fixtures and Furnishings

A Ball Plumbing Supply
1703 W. Burnside
Portland, OR 97209
(503) 228-0026

Amerec Corp.
Box 3825
Bellevue, WA 98009
(800) 426-0848

American Olean Tile Co.
1000 Cannon Ave.
Lansdale, PA 19446
(215) 855-1711

American-Standard
Box 2003
New Brunswick, NJ 08903
(201) 885-1900

Artistic Brass
4100 Ardmore Ave.
South Gate, CA 90280
(213) 564-1100

Laura Ashley
Box 5308
Melville, NY 11747
(800) 523-6383

California Cooperage
Box E
San Luis Obispo, CA 93406
(805) 544-9300

Decorative Hardware Studio
160 King St.
Chappaqua, NY 10514
(914) 238-5220

Delta Faucet Co.
Box 40980, 55 E. 111th St.
Indianapolis, IN 46280
(317) 848-1812

Eljer Plumbingware
Wallace Murray Corp.
3 Gateway Ctr.
Pittsburgh, PA 15222
(412) 553-7200

Elon Inc.
642 Sawmill River Rd.
Ardsley, NY 10502
(914) 693-8000

General Marble Corp.
9507 Arrow
Rancho Cucamonga, CA
  91730
(800) 854-7957
In CA: (714) 987-4636

Grohe America Inc.
2677 Coyle Ave.
Elk Grove Village, IL 60007
(312) 640-6650

P. E. Guerin Inc.
23 Jane St.
New York, NY 10014
(212) 243-5270

Hastings Tile & Il Bagno
  Collection
410 Lakeville Rd.
Lake Success, NY 11042
(516) 328-8600

Italbagno
1 NE 40th St.
Miami, FL 33140
(305) 573-4507

Jacuzzi Whirlpool Bath Inc.
298 N. Wiget Lane
Walnut Creek, CA 94596
(415) 938-7070

Kohler Co.
517 Highland Dr.
Kohler, WI 53044
(414) 451-4141

Random & Width
Box 427
West Chester, PA 19380
(215) 436-4632

Renovator's Supply Inc.
Millers Falls, MA 01349
(413) 659-3141

Smolka
182 Madison Ave.
New York, NY 10016
(212) 679-2700

Speakman Co.
301 E. 30th St.
Wilmington, DE 19899
(302) 764-7100

Sunrise Specialty
2210 San Pablo Ave.
Berkeley, CA 94702
(415) 845-4751

Vermont Marble Co.
61 Main St.
Proctor, VT 05765
(802) 459-3311

Sherle Wagner
60 E. 57th St.
New York, NY 10022
(212) 688-1150

Walker Industries
Box 129
Bellevue, TN 37221
(615) 646-5084

Walker & Zanger
Box 241
Scarsdale, NY 10583
(914) 472-5666

Watercolors Inc.
Garrison-on-Hudson, NY
  10524
(914) 424-3327

Waterworks
179 South St.
Boston, MA 02111
(617) 482-8811

Westchester Marble &
  Granite Inc.
179 Summerfield St.
Scarsdale, NY 10583
(914) 472-5666

Whitehead Studios
210 S. Clinton St.
Chicago, IL 60606
(312) 454-9046

Cabinets

Allmilmo Corp.
Box 629
Fairfield, NJ 07006
(201) 227-2502

Aristokraft
14th and Aristokraft Sq.
Box 420
Jasper, IN 47546
(812) 482-2527

Atlantic Cabinet Corp.
Interstate Pike, Box 100
Williamsport, MD 21795
(301) 223-8900

Breakfast Woodworks Inc.
50 Maple St.
Branford, CT 06405
(203) 488-8364

Fife's Woodworking &
  Manufacturing Co., Inc.
9 Main St.
Northwood, NH 03261
(603) 942-8339

Formica Corp.
One Cyanamid Plaza
Wayne, NJ 07470
(201) 831-4174

Keller
18000 State Rd. 9
Miami, FL 33162
(305) 651-7100

Kitchen Kompact
KK Plaza, Box 868
Jeffersonville, IN 47131
(812) 282-6681

William Lyons Design Craft,
  Inc.
41-21 28th St.
Long Island City, NY 11101
(212) 786-0661

Macor, Inc.
801 N. State St.
Elgin, IL 60120
(312) 697-3333

Merillat Industries, Inc.
Box 1946
Adrian, MI 49221
(517) 263-0771

Poggenpohl USA Corp.
222 Cedar Ln.
Teaneck, NJ 07666
(201) 836-1550

Robern Inc.
1766 Winchester Rd.
Bensalem, PA 19020
(215) 245-6550

Dennis Paul Robillard
Front St.
South Berwick, ME 03908
(207) 384-9541

Rutt Custom Kitchens
Rte. 23
Goodville, PA 17528
(215) 445-6751

St. Charles Manufacturing
Co.
St. Charles, IL 60174
(312) 584-3800

Wood Mode Cabinetry
Kreamer, PA 17833
(717) 374-2711

The Woodstone Co.
Box 223, Patch Rd.
Westminster, VT 05158
(802) 722-4784

Flooring

Agency Tile Inc.
499 Old Nyack Tpke
Spring Valley, NY 10977
(914) 352-7620

American Olean Tile Co.
1000 Cannon Ave.
Lansdale, PA 19446
(215) 855-1111

Armstrong World Industries
Inc.
Box 3001
Lancaster, PA 17604
(717) 397-0611

Laura Ashley
Box 5308
Melville, NY 11747
(800) 523-6383

Bruce Hardwood Floors
16803 Dallas Pkwy
Box 220100
Dallas, TX 75248
(214) 931-3000

Congoleum Corp.
195 Belgrove Dr.
Kearny, NJ 07032
(201) 991-1000

Country Floors, Inc.
300 E. 61st St.
New York, NY 10021
(212) 758-7414

Craftsman Lumber Co.
Box 222
Groton, MA 01450
(617) 448-6336

Delaware Quarries Inc.
River Rd.
Lumberville, PA 18933
(215) 297-5647

Depot Woodworking Inc.
683 Pine St.
Burlington, VT 05401
(802) 658-5670

Elon, Inc.
642 Sawmill River Rd.
Ardsley, NY 10502
(914) 693-8000

Florida Tile
Box 447
Lakeland, FL 33802
(813) 687-7171

Forms & Surfaces
Box 5215
Santa Barbara, CA 93108
(805) 969-5033

Franciscan Ceramic Tile
2901 Los Feliz Blvd.
Los Angeles, CA 90039
(213) 663-3361

Fresh Impressions Inc.
882 Rte. 22
Somerville, NJ 08876
(201) 526-5353

Gaf Corp.
140 W 51st St.
New York, NY 10020
(212) 621-5000

H & R Johnson Tiles Ltd.
Highgate Tile Works
Tunstall, Stoke-on-Trent
Staffordshire ST6 4JX
England

Kentucky Wood Floors, Inc.
4200 Reservoir Ave.
Louisville, KY 40213
(502) 451-6024

Magnum Marble
147 Larchmont Ave.
Larchmont, NY 10538
(914) 833-0305

Mannington Mills Inc.
Box 30
Salem, NJ 08079
(609) 935-3000

Maurer & Shepherd Joyners
Inc.
122 Naubuc Ave.
Glastonbury, CT 06033
(203) 633-2383

Natural Vinyl Floor Co.,
Inc.
4401 Mars Hill Rd.
Box 1302
Florence, AL 35631
(800) 633-3380
In AL: (205) 767-4990

Parma Tile Mosaic &
Marble Co., Inc.
14-38 Astoria Blvd.
Long Island City, NY 11102
(212) 278-3060

Taos Clay Products Inc.
Box 15
Taos, NM 87571
(515) 758-9513

Tibbals Flooring Co.
Oneida, TN 37841
(615) 569-8526

U.S. Brick
Box 66
Corunna, MI 48817
(517) 743-3444

Vermont Marble Co.
61 Main St.
Proctor, VT 05765
(802) 459-3311

Westchester Marble &
Granite Inc.
179 Summerfield St.
Scarsdale, NY 10583
(914) 472-5666

Greenhouses

Abundant Energy
116 Newport Bridge Rd.
Warwick, NY 10990
(914) 258-4022

Advance Energy
Technologies
Box 387
Clifton Park, NY 12065
(518) 371-2140

AFG Industries
Box 929
Kingsport, TN 37662
(615) 245-0211

Aluminum Greenhouses,
Inc.
14605 Lorain Ave.
Cleveland, OH 44111
(216) 251-6100

Barrel Builders
1085 Lodi Ln.
St. Helena, CA 94574
(707) 963-7914

Brady & Sun
97 Webster St.
Worcester, MA 01603
(617) 755-9580

Charley's Greenhouse
Supply
12815 NE 124th St.
Kirkland, WA 98033
(208) 823-1616

English Greenhouse
Products Corp.
11th & Linden Sts.
Camden, NJ 08102
(609) 966-6161

Garden Way Research
Charlotte, VT 05445
(802) 425-2137

Green Mountain Homes
Royalton, VT 05068
(802) 762-8384

Habitat Specialty Buildings
123 Elm St.
South Deerfield, MA 01373
(413) 665-4006

Hasco Industries
10 Park Ave.
West Orange, NJ 07052
(201) 736-9550

Lantz Enterprises
1373 Howell Dr.
Newark, OH 43055
(614) 344-6600

Lord & Burnham
Irvington, NY 10533
(914) 591-8800

Northern Sun
21705 Hwy 99
Lynwood, WA 98036
(206) 771-3334

Princeton Energy Group
575 Ewing St.
Princeton, NJ 08540
(609) 921-1965

Sierra Greenhouse
2419-A Mercantile Dr.
Rancho Cordova, CA 95670
(916) 638-1884

Solar Additions
15 W. Main St.
Cambridge, NY 12816
(518) 677-3700

Solar Components
Box 237
Manchester, NH 03105
(603) 668-8186

Sun System
60M Vanderbilt Motor
Pkwy.
Commack, NY 11725
(800) 645-4506
In NY: (516) 543-7766

Sunsitive Systems
365 East Park Ave.
Long Beach, NY 11561
(516) 431-1059

Sunwrights
334 Washington St.
Somerville, MA 02143
(617) 628-5030

Thermodular Designs, Inc.
5095 Paris St.
Denver, CO 80239
(303) 371-4111

Vegetable Factory, Inc.
100 Court St.
Copiague, NY 11726
(516) 842-9300

Wasco Products, Inc.
Box 351
Sanford, ME 04073
(207) 324-8060

Hardware

Baldwin Hardware
  Manufacturing Corp.
841 Wyomissing Blvd.
Box 82
Reading, PA 19603
(215) 777-7811

Blaine Window Hardware
  Inc.
1919 Blaine Dr., RD 4
Hagerstown, MD 21740
(301) 797-6500

Julius Blum & Co., Inc.
Box 292
Carlstadt, NJ 07072
(201) 438-4600

Cirecast, Inc.
380 7th St.
San Francisco, CA 94103
(415) 863-8319

Crawford's Old House Store
301 McCall
Waukesha, WI 53186
(414) 542-0685

The Decorative Hardware
  Studio
160 King St.
Chappaqua, NY 10514
(914) 238-5251

Forms & Surfaces
Box 5215
Santa Barbara, CA 93108
(805) 969-4767

Heinze America Ltd.
322B Edwardia Dr.
Greensboro, NC 27409
(919) 852-0000

Horton Brasses
Nooks Hill Rd., Box 95
Cromwell, CT 06416
(203) 635-4400

Kwikset
516 Santa Ana St.
Anaheim, CA 92803
(714) 535-8111

Nutone
Madison & Red Bank Rds.
Cincinnati, OH 45227
(513) 527-5100

Pfanstiel Hardware Co., Inc.
Jeffersonville, NY 12748
(914) 482-4445

Random & Width
Box 427
West Chester, PA 19380
(215) 436-4632

Renaissance Decorative
  Hardware Co.
Box 332
Leonia, NJ 07605
(201) 568-1403

Ritter & Son Hardware
Gualala, CA 95445
(800) 358-9120
In CA: (800) 862-4948

Schlage Lock Co.
2401 Bayshore Blvd.
San Francisco, CA 94134
(415) 467-1100

Walker & Zanger, Inc.
Box 241
Scarsdale, NY 10583
(914) 472-5666

Vincent Whitney Co.
Box 335
Sausalito, CA 94965
(415) 332-3260

The Woodworkers' Store
21801 Industrial Blvd.
Rogers, MN 55374
(612) 428-4101

Appropriate Technology
 Corp.
Box 975
Brattleboro, VT 05301
(802) 257-4501

Bryant Air Conditioning
7310 W. Morris St.
Indianapolis, IN 46231
(317) 243-0851

Carrier Air Conditioning
Box 4808, Carrier Pkwy.
Syracuse, NY 13221
(315) 432-6000

Ceramic Radiant Heat
Pleasant Dr.
Lochmere, NH 03252
(603) 524-9663

Empire Furnace & Stove
 Repair Co.
793-97 Broadway
Albany, NY 12207
(518) 449-5189

Energy Marketing Corp.
Box 636
Bennington, VT 05301
(802) 442-8513

Friedrich Air Conditioning
 & Refrigeration Co.
4200 N. Pan Am Expwy.
San Antonio, TX 78295
(512) 225-2000

General Electric Co.
Appliance Park, Bldg. 6
Louisville, KY 40225
(502) 452-4971

Grandpa's Wood Stoves
Box 492
Ware, MA 01082
(413) 967-6684

Grumman Energy Systems
 Inc.
445 Broadhollow Rd.
Melville, NY 11747
(516) 454-8600

Honeywell Inc.
10400 Yellow Circle Dr.
Minnetonka, MN 55343
(612) 931-4142

Lehman's Hardware &
 Appliances, Inc.
Box 41
Kidron, OH 44636
(216) 857-5441

Lennox Industries
Box 400450
Dallas, TX 75240
(214) 783-5452

Majestic
1000 E. Market St.
Huntington, IN 46750
(219) 356-8000

McGraw-Edison Co.
1701 Golf Rd.
Rolling Meadows, IL 60008
(312) 981-3800

Owens-Corning Fiberglas
 Corp.
Fiberglas Tower
Toledo, OH 43659
(419) 248-8000

Sunsitive Systems
365 East Park Ave.
Long Beach, NY 11561
(516) 431-1059

Upland Stove Co.
2 Green St., Box 87
Greene, NY 13778
(607) 656-4156

Woodstock Soapstone Co.,
 Inc.
Rte 4, Box 223
Woodstock, VT 05091
(802) 672-5133

York
Box 1592
York, PA 17405
(717) 846-7890

Kitchen and Laundry Fixtures and Furnishings

American Olean Tile Co.
1000 Cannon Ave.
Lansdale, PA 19446
(215) 855-1711

American-Standard
Box 2003
New Brunswick, NJ 08903
(201) 885-1900

ARD Custom Kitchens &
 Baths
No. 1 Fourth Pl.
Brooklyn, NY 11231
(212) 624-5688

Laura Ashley
Box 5308
Melville, NY 11747
(800) 523-6383

Atag USA Corp.
2605 Broadway Ave.
Evanston, IL 60201
(312) 869-1900

Brookstone Co.
127 Vose Farm Rd.
Peterborough, NH 03458
(603) 924-7181

Chambers Corp.
Box 927
Oxford, MS 38655
(601) 234-3131

Chicago Faucet Co.
2100 S. Nuclear Dr.
Des Plaines, IL 60018
(312) 694-4400

Dwyer Products Corp.
Calumet Ave.
Michigan City, IN 46360
(219) 874-5236

Frigidaire Co.
Box W.C. 4900
3555 S. Kettering Blvd.
Dayton, OH 45449
(513) 297-3400

Grohe America
2677 Coyle Ave.
Elk Grove Village, IL 60007
(312) 640-6650

Hastings Tile & Il Bagno
  Collection
410 Lakeville Rd.
Lake Success, NY 11042
(516) 328-8600

Hotpoint
2100 Gardiner Ln., Suite 301
Louisville, KY 40205
(502) 452-5364

In-Sink-Erator
4700 21st St.
Racine, WI 53406
(414) 554-5432

Jenn-Air Corp.
3035 Shadeland Dr.
Indianapolis, IN 46226
(317) 545-2271

KitchenAid
World Headquarters
Troy, OH 45374
(513) 335-7171

Kohler Co.
High St.
Kohler, WI 53004
(414) 457-4441

Maytag Co.
403 W. 4th St. N.
Newton, IA 50208
(515) 792-7000

Modern Maid
Box 111
Chattanooga, TN 37401
(615) 624-2661

Moen
377 Woodland Ave.
Elyria, OH 44036
(216) 323-3341

Mutschler
302 S. Madison St.
Nappanee, IN 46550
(219) 773-3111

Nutone
Madison & Red Bank Rds.
Cincinnati, OH 45227
(513) 527-5100

Rutt Custom Kitchens
Rte. 23
Goodville, PA 17528
(215) 445-6751

Scotsman Ice Systems
505 Front St.
Albert Lea, MN 56007
(507) 373-3961

Sharp Electronics Corp.
10 Sharp Plaza
Paramus, NJ 07652
(201) 265-5600

Sub-Zero Freezer Co., Inc.
4717 Hammersley Rd.,
Box 4130
Madison, WI 53711
(608) 271-2233

Thermador/Waste King
5119 District Blvd.
Los Angeles, CA 90040
(213) 562-1133

Union Woodworks/Wall-
  Goldfinger
7 Belknap St.
Northfield, VT 05663
(802) 485-6161

Vermont Marble Co.
61 Main St.
Proctor, VT 05765
(802) 459-3311

Walker & Zanger
Box 241
Scarsdale, NY 10583
(914) 472-5666

Waterworks
179 South St.
Boston, MA 02111
(617) 482-8811

Westchester Marble &
  Granite, Inc.
179 Summerfield St.
Box 241
Scarsdale, NY 10583
(914) 472-5666

Whirlpool
Benton Harbor, MI 49022
(616) 926-5000

Whitehead Studios
210 S. Clinton St.
Chicago, IL 60606
(312) 454-9046

White-Westinghouse
930 Ft. Duquesne
Pittsburgh, PA 15222
(412) 263-3725

The Woodworker's Store
21801 Industrial Blvd.
Rogers, MN 55374
(612) 420-4101

Lighting Fixtures

Artemide, Inc.
150 E. 58th St.
New York, NY 10155
(212) 980-0710

Boyd Lighting Co.
56 12th St.
San Francisco, CA 94103
(415) 431-4300

The Classic Illumination
431 Grove St.
Oakland, CA 94607
(415) 465-7786

Devoe Lighting Corp.
800 Eastern Ave.
Carlstadt, NJ 07072
(201) 935-2300

General Electric Co.
Lighting Systems Dept.
Hendersonville, NC 28739
(704) 693-2200

Illuminating Experiences,
    Inc.
107 Trumbull St.
Elizabeth, NJ 07206
(201) 527-8847

ITT Indoor Lighting
Box 195
Vermilion, OH 44089
(216) 967-3131

Koch & Lowy, Inc.
21-24 39th Ave.
Long Island City, NY 11101
(212) 786-3520

George Kovacs Lighting Inc.
24 W. 40th St.
New York, NY 10018
(212) 944-9606

Lighting Associates, Inc.
305 E. 63rd St.
New York, NY 10021
(212) 751-0575

Lightolier, Inc.
346 Claremont Ave.
Jersey City, NJ 07305
(201) 333-5120

Metropolitan Lighting
    Fixture Co.
1010 Third Ave.
New York, NY 10021
(212) 838-2425

Nessen Lamps Inc.
621 E. 216th St.
Bronx, NY 10467
(212) 231-0221

Nutone
Madison & Red Bank Rds.
Cincinnati, OH 45227
(513) 527-5100

Plexability, Ltd.
200 Lexington Ave.
New York, NY 10016
(212) 679-7826

Renovator's Supply, Inc.
Millers Falls, MA 01349
(413) 659-3141

Thunder & Light
147 41st St.
Brooklyn, NY 11232
(212) 499-3777

Wasley Lighting Inc.
Plains Rd.
Essex, CT 06426
(800) 243-8194
In CT: (203) 767-0191

Welsbach Lighting
240 Sargent Dr.
New Haven, CT 06511
(203) 789-1710

Bendix Mouldings Inc.
235 Pegasus Ave.
Northvale, NJ 07647
(201) 767-8888

Breakfast Woodworks, Inc.
50 Maple St.
Branford, CT 06405
(203) 488-8364

Classic Moulders
911 Railroad Ave.
West Palm Bach, FL 33401
(305) 659-4200

Creative Additions Ltd.
79 Madison Ave.
New York, NY 10016
(212) 679-1515

Cumberland Woodcraft
  Company Inc.
2500 Walnut Bottom Rd.
Carlisle, PA 17013
(717) 243-0063

The Decorators Supply
  Corp.
3610-12 S. Morgan St.
Chicago, IL 60609
(312) 847-6300

Depot Woodworking Inc.
683 Pine St.
Burlington, VT 05401
(802) 658-5670

Entasis Ltd.
32 Jones St.
New York, NY 10014
(212) 255-5185

Focal Point Inc.
2005 Marietta Rd. NW
Atlanta, GA 30318
(404) 351-0820

Haas Wood and Ivory Works
64 Clementina St.
San Francisco, CA 94105
(415) 421-8273

Industrial Woodworking,
  Inc.
1331 Leithton Rd.
Mundelein, IL 60060
(312) 367-9080

William Lyon Design Craft,
  Inc.
41-21 28th St.
Long Island City, NY 11101
(212) 786-0661

Maurer & Shepherd Joyners
  Inc.
122 Naubuc Ave.
Glastonbury, CT 06033
(203) 633-2383

Rosewood Ventures
Box 610
Port Maitland, Yarmouth
  County
Nova Scotia, Canada
  B0W 2V0
(902) 649-2782

Star Moulding & Trim Co.
6606 W. 74th St.
Bedford Park, IL 60638
(312) 458-1040

Urban Archaeology
137 Spring St.
New York, NY 10012
(212) 431-6969

Wall Goldfinger Design
  Associates
7 Belknap St.
Northfield, VT 05663
(802) 485-6261

The Woodstone Company
 Box 223, Patch Rd.
Westminster, VT 05158
(802) 722-4784

Patio and Paving Materials; Decking

Architectural Terra Cotta
  and Tile, Ltd.
932 W. Washington St.
Chicago, IL 60607
(312) 666-1181

C I Designs
574 Boston Ave., Box 191
Medford, MA 02155
(617) 391-7800

Colonial Brick Co.
3344 W. Cermak Rd.
Chicago, IL 60623
(312) 927-0700

Glen-Gery Corp.
Box 280, Rte. 61
Shoemakersville, PA 19555
(215) 652-3076

Old Colonial Brick Co.
Majolica Rd.
Salisbury, NC 28144
(704) 636-8850

Osmose Wood Preserving
  Co. of America, Inc.
980 Ellicott St.
Buffalo, NY 14209
(716) 882-5905

Pascack Valley Stone &
Slate Co., Inc.
400 Demarest Ave.
Closter, NJ 07624
(201) 768-2133

Rising & Nelson Slate Co.,
Inc.
West Pawlet, VT 05775
(802) 645-0150

Royal River Brick Co.
Box 458
Gray, ME 04039
(207) 657-4498

The Structural Slate Co.
Pen Argyl, PA 18072
(215) 862-4141

U. S. Brick
Box 66
Corunna, MI 48817
(517) 743-3444

Vermont Marble Co.
61 Main St.
Proctor, VT 05765
(802) 459-3311

Vermont Structural Slate Co.
Box 98
Fair Haven, VT 05743
(802) 265-4933

Westchester Marble &
Granite Inc.
179 Summerfield St.
Scarsdale, NY 10583
(914) 472-5666

Railings and Columns

Amherst Woodworking &
Supply, Inc.
Box 575, Hubbard Ave.
Northampton, MA 01061
(413) 584-3003

Bendix Mouldings, Inc.
235 Pegasus Ave.
Northvale, NJ 07647
(800) 526-0240
In NJ: (201) 767-8888

Elk Valley Woodworking
Co.
Rte 1, Box 23
Carter, OK 73627
(405) 486-3337

Haas Wood and Ivory Works
64 Clementina St.
San Francisco, CA 94105
(415) 421-8273

Mad River Wood Works
4935 Boyd Rd., Box 163
Arcata, CA 95521
(707) 826-0629

Michael's Fine Colonial
Products
Rte. 44, RD 1 Box 179A
Salt Point, NY 12578
(914) 677-3960

A. F. Schwerd Manufactur-
ing Co.
3215 McClure Ave.
Pittsburgh, PA 15212
(412) 766-6322

Somerset Door & Column
Co.
S. Edgewood Ave., Box 328
Somerset, PA 15501
(814) 445-9608

Roofing

Alcoa Building Products,
Inc.
2 Allegheny Ctr., Suite 1200
Pittsburgh, PA 15212
(412) 553-3026

Architectural Terra Cotta
and Tile, Ltd.
932 W. Washington St.
Chicago, IL 60607
(312) 666-1181

Celotex Corp.
1500 N. Dale Mabry
Tampa, FL 33607
(813) 871-4510

CY/RO Industries
697 Rte. 46
Clifton, NJ 07015
(201) 365-6700

General Electric Co.
3135 Easton Tpke.
Fairfield, CT 06431
(203) 373-2101

Ludowici-Celadon
Divison of CSC Inc.
Box 69
New Lexington, OH 43764
(614) 342-1995

Mad River Woodworks
Box 163
Arcata, CA 95521
(707) 826-0629

Masonite Corp.
29 N. Wacker Dr.
Chicago, IL 60606
(312) 372-5642

Renovator's Supply Inc.
Millers Falls, MA 01349
(413) 659-3141

Shakertown Corp.
Box 400
Winlock, WA 98956
(206) 785-3501

Sun Valle Tile Kilns
1717 N. Highland Ave.
Los Angeles, CA 90028
(213) 464-7289

Supradur Manufacturing
    Corp.
122 E. 42nd St.
New York, NY 10017
(212) 697-1160

Weyerhaeuser Co.
Tacoma, WA 98401
(206) 924-2345

Skylights and Roof Windows

Andersen Corp.
Bayport, MN 55003
(612) 770-7212

APC Corp.
50 Utter Ave.
Hawthorne, NJ 07507
(201) 423-2900

Bristol Fiberlite Industries
401 E. Goetz Ave.
Santa Ana, CA 92707
(714) 540-8950

The Condon Studios
33 Richdale Ave.
Cambridge, MA 02140
(617) 661-5776

Cyro Industries
Box 8588
Woodcliff Lake, NJ 07675
(800) 631-5384

Dawn Products Co.
Box 1003, 5251 S. Rio
    Grande
Littleton, CO 80160
(303) 795-0908

James B. Furman Glass
    Studio
27 W. Main St.
Trumansburg, NY 14886
(607) 387-4141

Hasco Industries
10 Park Ave.
West Orange, NJ 07052
(201) 736-9550

Kennedy Sky-Lites Corp.
3647 All American Blvd.
Orlando, FL 32810
(305) 293-3880

Naturalite, Inc.
3233 W. Kingsley Rd.
Garland, TX 75041
(214) 278-1354

ODL Inc.
215 E. Roosevelt Ave.
Zeeland, MI 49464
(616) 772-9111

O'Keefe's Inc.
75 Williams Ave.
San Francisco, CA 94124
(415) 822-4222

Paeco Inc.
1 Executive Dr.
Toms River, NJ 08753
(201) 341-4444

Rohm & Haas Co.
Independence Mall W.
Philadelphia, PA 19105
(215) 592-3000

Rollomatic Roofs Inc.
1400 Yosemite Ave.
San Francisco, CA 94124
(415) 822-5655

Skyline Products
2903 Delta Dr.
Colorado Springs, CO 80910
(303) 392-4228

Skymaster
413 Virginia Dr.
Orlando, FL 32803
(305) 898-2881

Sunsitive Systems
365 E. Park Ave.
Long Beach, NY 11561
(516) 431-1059

Velux-America, Inc.
Box 3208
Greenwood, SC 29646
(803) 223-4281

Ventarama Skylight Corp.
140 Cantiague Rock Rd.
Hicksville, NY 11801
(516) 931-0202

Wasco Products, Inc.
Box 351
Sanford, ME 04073
(207) 324-8060

Stairways

Architectural Paneling Inc.
979 Third Ave.
New York, NY 10022
(212) 371-9632

Baluchi Marble Ltd.
8687 Melrose Ave., Suite
432
Los Angeles, CA 90069
(213) 659-3832

Barewood Inc.
141 Atlantic Ave.
Brooklyn, NY 11207
(212) 875-3833

Cooper Stair Co.
1331 Leithton Rd.
Mundelein, IL 60060
(312) 362-8800

Mansion Industries
14711 E. Clark
City of Industry, CA 91745
(213) 968-9501

Midwest Spiral Stair
2153 W. Division St.
Chicago, IL 60622
(800) 621-3886
In IL: (312) 227-8461

Mylen Industries
650 Washington St.
Peekskill, NY 10566
(800) 431-2155
In NY: (914) 739-8486
(212) 585-6767

Puccio/European Marble
Works, Inc.
232 E. 59th St.
New York, NY 10021
(212) 688-1351

Rambusch
40 W. 13th St.
New York, NY 10011
(212) 675-0400

Stair Specialist
2257 W. Columbia Ave.
Battle Creek, MI 49017
(616) 964-2351

The Woodworker's Store
21801 Industrial Blvd.
Rogers, MN 55374
(612) 420-4101

York Spiral Stair
N. Vassalboro, ME 04962
(207) 872-5558

Storage: Closets, Shelving

Carriage House Showrooms,
Inc.
180 NE 39th St.
Miami, FL 33137
(305) 576-1264

Closet Systems Corp.
1175 Broadway
Hewlett, NY 11557
(516) 569-1400

Custom-Art Furniture
Max Durst Inc.
225 E. 24th St.
New York, NY 10010
(212) 684-4465

Dux
305 E. 63rd St.
New York, NY 10021
(212) 752-3897

Ello Furniture Manufacturing Co.
1034 Elm St.
Rockford, IL 61101
(815) 964-8601

Luxurious Laminates
Box 325
Pine Island, NY 10969
(914) 258-4841

Cy Mann Designs Ltd.
979 Third Ave.
New York, NY 10022
(212) 758-6830

Mondrian Inc.
1021 2nd Ave.
New York, NY 10022
(212) EL 5-7373

Poggenpohl USA Corp.
222 Cedar Lane, #305
Teaneck, NJ 07666
(201) 836-1550

St. Charles Manufacturing
Co.
St. Charles, IL 60174
(312) 584-3800

Sunar
18 Marshall St.
Norwalk, CT 06854
(203) 866-3100

Walls and Insulation

American Olean Tile Co.
1000 Cannon Ave.
Lansdale, PA 19446
(215) 855-1711

Architectural Terra Cotta
and Tile, Ltd.
932 W. Washington St.
Chicago, IL 60607
(312) 666-1181

Berkshire Porcelain Studios
Deerfield Ave.
Shelburne Falls, MA 10370
(413) 625-9447

CertainTeed Corp.
Box 860
Valley Forge, PA 19482
(215) 687-5000

Franciscan Ceramic Tile
2901 Los Feliz Blvd.
Los Angeles, CA 90039
(213) 663-3361

H & R Johnson Tiles Ltd.
Highgate Tile Works
Tunstall, Stoke-on-Trent
England ST6 4JX

Hastings Tile & Il Bagno
Collection
410 Lakeville Rd.
Lake Success, NY 11042
(516) 328-8600

Parma Tile Mosaic &
Marble Co., Inc.
14-38 Astoria Blvd.
Long Island City, NY 11102
(212) 278-3060

Pittsburgh Corning Corp.
800 Presque Isle Dr.
Pittsburgh, PA 15239
(412) 327-6100

Taos Clay Products
Box 15
Taos, NM 87571
(505) 758-9513

U. S. Brick
Box 66
Corunna, MI 48817
(517) 743-3444

U.S. Gypsum Co.
101 S. Wacker Dr.
Chicago, IL 60606
(312) 321-4122

Vermont Marble Co.
61 Main St.
Proctor, VT 05765
(802) 459-3311

Walker & Zanger
Box 241
Scarsdale, NY 10583
(914) 472-5666

Westchester Marble &
Granite Inc.
179 Summerfield St.
Scarsdale, NY 10583
(914) 472-5666

Whitehead Studios
210 S. Clinton St.
Chicago, IL 60606
(312) 454-9046

Windows and Doors

Acorn Building Components
12620 Westwood Avenue
Detroit, MI 48223
(313) 272-5700

Alcan Building Products
Box 511
Warren, OH 44482
(216) 841-3460

Andersen Corp.
Bayport, MN 55003
(612) 770-7212

Architectural Components
Box 246
Leverett, MA 01054
(413) 549-1094

Barewood Inc.
141 Atlantic Ave.
Brooklyn, NY 11207
(212) 875-3833

Biltbest Windows
175 Coyne St.
Ste. Genevieve, MO 63670
(314) 883-3575

Breakfast Woodworks, Inc.
50 Maple St.
Branford, CT 06405
(203) 488-8364

Capitol Windows
Ethyl Capitol Products
Box 3070
Harrisburg, PA 17105
(717) 766-7661

Caradco
Box 920
Rantoul, IL 61866
(217) 893-4444

The Condon Studios
33 Richdale Ave.
Cambridge, MA 02140
(617) 661-5776

Duratherm Window Corp.
North Vassalboro, ME
  04962
(207) 872-5558

The Emporium
2515 Morse St.
Houston, TX 77019
(713) 528-3808

James B. Furman Glass
  Studio
27 W. Main St.
Trumansburg, NY 14886
(607) 387-4141

General Products Co., Inc.
Box 7387
Fredericksburg, VA 22404
(703) 898-5700

International Wood Products
9630 Aero Dr.
San Diego, CA 92128
(714) 565-1122

Keller
18000 State Rd. 9
Miami, FL 33162
(305) 651-7100

Keystone Wood Specialties
31 S. Ronks Rd.
Ronks, PA 17572
(800) 233-0289
In PA: (717) 687-6340

Marni Bakst Leaded Glass
235 E. 5th St.
New York, NY 10003
(212) 533-2556

Marvin Windows
Warroad, MN 56763
(218) 386-1430

Maurer & Shepherd Joyners
  Inc.
122 Naubuc Ave.
Glastonbury, CT 06033
(203) 633-2383

Michael's Fine Colonial
  Products
Rte. 44, RD 1 Box 179A
Salt Point, NY 12578
(914) 677-3960

C.E. Morgan
Box 2446
Oshkosh, WI 54903
(414) 235-7170

Noranda Aluminum
  Building Products
7120 Krick Rd.
Cleveland, OH 44146
(216) 232-5500

Norco Windows, Inc.
Box 309
Hawkins, WI 54530
(715) 585-6311

Peachtree Doors, Inc.
Box 5700
Norcross, GA 30091
(404) 449-0880

Pella/Rolscreen Co.
100 Main St.
Pella, Iowa 50219
(515) 628-1000

Pittsburgh Corning Corp.
800 Presque Isle Dr.
Pittsburgh, PA 15239
(412) 327-6100

Pozzi Window Co.
Box 5249
Bend, OR 97708
(800) 597-6880

Remodelers' & Renovators'
  Supply
611 E. 44th St.
Boise, ID 83704
(208) 377-5465

Rosewood Ventures
Box 610
Port Maitland, Yarmouth
  County
Nova Scotia, Canada
  B0W 2V0
(902) 649-2782

Weather Shield
  Manufacturing Inc.
Box 309
Medford, WI 54451
(715) 748-2100

The Woodstone Co.
Box 223, Patch Rd.
Westminster, VT 05158
(802) 722-4784

ACKNOWLEDGMENTS

This book is the result of the combined assistance of many people to whom I am indebted. While surveying residential additions in the United States and Canada, I contacted nearly 250 architectural firms. I appreciate their sending me 150 projects to review for the book. Researching and writing about the 30 projects I selected could not have happened without the diligent and energetic aid of Holland Sweet. Finally, the enthusiastic assistance of Lawrence Grow and Frank Mahood of The Main Street Press is gratefully acknowledged.

PHOTO CREDITS

Frontispiece: Ron Shuller
Chapter 1. Valerie Walsh
Chapter 2. Beth Facinelli
Chapter 3. Joe Hylton
Chapter 4. Langdon Clay
Chapter 5. Ervin Addy
Chapter 6. Ron Shuller
Chapter 7. Bert Stern
Chapter 8. Michael Slack
Chapter 9. Glen Jarvis
Chapter 10. Larry Carpp
Chapter 11. James Oleg Kruhly

Chapter 12. Architectural Design Group
Chapter 13. James W. Krengel
Chapter 14. Glen Jarvis
Chapter 15. Stephen Lasar
Chapter 16. James Oleg Kruhly
Chapter 17. Robert Perron
Chapter 18. Eric Meola
Chapter 19. Leslie Armstrong
Chapter 20. Ron Gordon
Chapter 21. Jefferson Riley
Chapter 22. William Mills

Chapter 23. Ernest Braun
Chapter 24. John Perry
Chapter 25. Steve Simpson
Chapter 26. Sarah Montgomery
Chapter 27. Peter C. Kurth
Chapter 28. Edward Gaudy and James Hadley
Chapter 29. Stan Better
Chapter 30. Peter C. Kurth